the
DEATH
of
HOCKEY

or: how a bunch of guys
with too much money and
too little sense are killing
the greatest game on earth

JEFF Z. KLEIN and KARL-ERIC REIF

Macmillan Canada
Toronto

Canadian Cataloguing in Publication Data

Klein, Jeff Z.

The death of hockey, or How a bunch of guys with too much money and too little sense are killing the greatest game on earth

ISBN 0-7715-7622-6

1. National Hockey League. 2. Hockey. I. Reif, Karl-Eric. II. Title. III. Title: How a bunch of guys with too much money and too little sense are killing the greatest game on earth.

GV847.K534 1998   796.962'64   C98-931551-7

1 2 3 4 5 FP 02 01 00 99 98

Cover and text design by Stray Toaster
Cover photo by Jim Gund/*Sports Illustrated*

Every effort has been made to determine whether previously published material required reprint permissions, and to contact current copyright holders. The authors apologize for any errors, and will make any necessary corrections that are brought to our attention in future editions of this book.

Excerpt on page 4 is extracted from *Barney's Version* by Mordecai Richler. ©1998. Reprinted by permission of Knopf Canada.

This book is available at special discounts for bulk purchases by your group or organization for sales promotions, premiums, fundraising and seminars. For details, contact: Macmillan Canada, Special Sales Department, 29 Birch Avenue, Toronto, ON M4V 1E2. Tel: 416-963-8830.

Macmillan Canada
A Division of Canada Publishing Corporation
Toronto, Ontario, Canada

Printed in Canada

We acknowledge the financial support of the Government of Canada through the Book Publishing Industry Development Program for our publishing activities.

For my roller hockey heroes,
Asher and Grace,
with all the love in the world.
—JZK

For Beth
—versatile tireless backbone of the team—
with love, gratitude, and admiration.
—KER

ACKNOWLEDGMENTS

Thanks to our agent, David Johnston at Livingston-Cooke, and to Alison Maclean at Macmillan for preparing a fine deal and an even better barbecue. And thanks to the crew at Macmillan for their fine work—Wendy Thomas for her eagle-eyed copy editing, Pierre LeBrun for his challenging hard read, and Meghan Brousseau for her ambitious promotion.

Thanks to John Morrison at The Hockey Information Service, Inc. and his terrific website for coming through in the frantic final seconds of play.

Thanks to all our friends and associates in the media for their insights and assistance, particularly everyone at *The New York Times* sports department and at *The New York Times Magazine*, and to the gang at Sports Information & Research for, ah, the information and research.

Thanks, as always, to our friends and families for their enthusiasm and encouragement—particularly Beth, who played secretary, errand-girl, proofreader, critic, and cheerleader. As if she had anything better to do!

Finally, our boundless appreciation to our editor at Macmillan, Susan Girvan, for her preternatural patience, energy, skill, and unfailing good humour. If we've all done our job well enough to create some positive effect, she may even become a hockey fan once again.

And as always, the authors thank each other.

JZK, New York City
KER, Buffalo

Contents

introduction

In 1994, the National Hockey League had it all: a new U.S. television contract with the burgeoning Fox Network and the national exposure it had sought for so long; a sweetheart champion in the media capital of the world, as the Rangers ended a 54-year Stanley Cup drought in a classic seven-game final; scores of dynamic, talented, wholesome star players thriving in a milieu free of the labour-management strife and drug and sex scandals that plagued baseball, football, and basketball. Hockey was finally poised to take its place as an equal member of the Big Four of North American sports, no longer to dwell as the perennial poor sister among their number.

Today, barely four years later, hockey is a mess. The quality of play is dull, drab, dismal. NHL teams, and the game itself, lack personality and excitement. Television ratings are down, and the game's most avid fans regard the current version of NHL hockey with frustration and indifference. Even Mario Lemieux, less than a year removed from winning a sixth scoring championship in the final season of his spectacular career, says at his induction into the Hockey Hall of Fame that he is glad to be retiring, that the NHL is boring. Dimly beginning to recognize the widespread crisis, the game's powers-that-be toss back and forth bizarre plans that would hideously alter the game's eternal, fundamental geometries. Hockey, the game that so recently had the sports world on its plate, is dying.

What happened? How did it all go so wrong?

We're here to examine the crisis hockey finds itself in, and how it got there. Like you, we're first and foremost just fans of the game—and we'd like to think we speak here on behalf of millions of fans who love hockey, but who also know it's in trouble, who are worried about the direction in which the game is headed, and who feel they have no voice to make their concerns heard.

Perhaps we should qualify that statement: we're *American* fans of the game. Well, pretty much, anyway. Both of us were born and raised in Buffalo, right across the river from you there in Canada. Growing up in a border city gives us a certain perspective on hockey, and on Canadian and American culture in general—not a better one, but a slightly different one, eh?

What you'll get from us here is our take on why hockey, the greatest game on earth, is now a horrible, tedious disaster; how it got that way; and how it can be saved. This isn't a ledger sheet detailing the inner financial workings of the league or a back-slapping round-up of insider opinions from the old boys' network. What it is, in various parts and various places, is a love letter, a lament, a history lesson, a blistering editorial, a sentimental journey, a media analysis, an autobiography, a bilious rant, a constructive criticism, a Socratic dialogue, a hopeful wish, and a call to arms. Or something.

Mainly it's a clearing house for all the complaints and criticisms that we and dozens of other sportswriters and analysts and countless thousands of fans have levelled at the NHL over the past couple of years or so, a place to gather those concerns, to weigh and examine them, and maybe get the voice of the fans heard in hockey's corridors of power.

It's been said that the best book is the one that tells you what you already know. If that's true, then we're sure you'll be satisfied with much of what we have to say—unless, of course, you're a National Hockey League executive. On the other hand, some truths are hard to take, and long-held assumptions go down hard. So a lot of what we have to say may challenge what you've been led to believe. Some of it may entertain you; some of it may upset you. But keep your sticks on the ice. Remember, we're saying all this because we love hockey as much as you do, and we hate what's being done to the game.

Chapter 1

paradise lost

> Saturday nights, providing the new, improved, no-talent,
> chickenshit Canadiens are in town, each one a multimillion-
> aire, Solange and I eat an early dinner at Pauzés, and then
> repair to the Forum, where once *nos glorieux* were just about
> invincible. My God, I remember when all they had to do was
> to leap over the boards in those red-and-white sweaters and
> the visiting team was a goner. Those, those were the days.
> Fire-wagon hockey. Soft but accurate passes. Fast-as-lightning
> wrist shots. Defencemen who could hit. And no ear-piercing
> rock music played at 10,000 decibels while a face-off was
> held up for a TV commercial.
>
> —Mordecai Richler, *Barney's Version*

Ask yourself, what are the best things about hockey? Think about that
for a minute. What elements of the game, what teams or players, what
sights or sounds, what fond memories or eager expectations make the
game special to you?

Every fan's list will be a little different; there would surely be no
consensus on the number one very best thing. Make your own list as
specific or as abstract as you like—persons, places, or things; a concept,
an image, a moment—the naked speed, or the heavy collisions, or the
booming shots... Paul Henderson's winning goal in the Summit Series,

or the manic joy of Theo Fleury's celebration after his overtime goal in the 1991 playoffs, or Dominik Hasek's game-saving stops in the 1998 Olympic shootout… the great player portraits in Maple Leaf Gardens, or the titanic portrait of the Queen in the Winnipeg Arena, or the hostesses in the Montreal Forum… the elemental sound of skates scraping ice, or the theme song from "Hockey Night in Canada"… the first pro game you ever attended, perhaps, or playing on the frozen backyard pond with your brothers or sisters, or with your own kids….

Veteran fans and newcomers will likely have some very different ideas, but as their lists, and yours, and ours, lengthen, a certain concordance, we think, would eventually appear. Before long we'd all have included somewhere on our list many of the same sights and sounds, the same stories and sensations. The best things about hockey are the things that make the game unique, that make it special, that, for you and us and all real fans of the game, make our memories and impressions of it so detailed and vivid, our passion for it so visceral, our hopes so high and our disappointments so crushing.

That passion for hockey isn't unique to Canadians; there are legions of fans in the United States, Scandinavia, central Europe, and Russia that love and appreciate the game. And a passion for our own particular sport isn't the sole province of hockey fans; baseball, football, basketball, soccer—you name the game—all have millions of fans just as crazy for their sport. But what is unique in hockey, what's unique in every sport, is what we would identify as the best things about it, the things that make it *different* from every other sport—its look and feel, its style and strategy, its characters, its history, its heritage.

In Canada, the game is always there. It's in the family, it's in the culture, it's in the air. Maybe you can still remember the first professional game you went to see, or the first time you played the game yourself. But you probably don't remember the first time you became aware of the game. It was always there. It was part of the natural environment, part of everyday experience from the day you were born.

Every fan discovers hockey in a different way and at a different time. How and when they discover the game gives each fan a slightly different perspective on it. And every fan comes to hockey with a different amount of experience and knowledge, a different degree of willingness to understand the game, and a different set of opportunities to learn about it. In the America of the 1950s and '60s, baseball had the kind of primacy that hockey has in Canada. And as kids growing up in the States in the '60s, even though we were just minutes from the Canadian border, hockey wasn't our first love or our only interest. We remember the first baseball game we went to, we remember the first time we swung a bat. But the first time we heard of baseball and knew what it meant, well, that's as lost to the mists of infancy as your memory or ours of the first time any of us ate ice cream or listened to a radio.

Hockey, though, was something we discovered almost by accident. We remember the first time we stumbled across it, on an afternoon telecast in the mid-1960s. And from that initial exposure, from that first glance, there was the same sense of wonder, the same shock of recognition, that only a handful of youthful experiences ever provides. It was one of those *this is the neatest thing I've ever seen* moments. Ice instead of grass? Skates instead of cleats? We don't want to sentimentalize the game or our discovery of it; it's been done for hockey, as it's been done endlessly for baseball. But the sights, the sounds, the textures—the speed, the collisions, the rasping of skates and the tapping of sticks on the ice, enclosed by echoing wooden boards topped then with metal mesh—those impressions are no less heady, no less important, for having since been spoken of and written about a thousand times.

Satisfied with the excitement of the game, we could have stopped there, remained entranced with the speed and collisions on the ice below, and taken no interest in how the game came to be what it was. But we wanted to learn everything we could about it. Our discovery of hockey, at that time and in that way, ignited our interest, and our drive to learn the game in the States in the late 1960s shaped the way we began to understand it.

Watching AHL games from the last row of the greys, then the top section of Buffalo's Memorial Auditorium, strengthened our fascination but added little to our knowledge of hockey's history. We took to trying to tune in "Hockey Night in Canada" from the Toronto station on a little black-and-white portable TV. Vague shadows drifted back and forth amid the snow and static, the action an almost indecipherable blur amid the crackling swarm of pixels. But the sound was clear, and while weekend homework sat untouched on the desk or on the floor, Danny Gallivan provided a weekly history lesson for us. While his polysyllabic warbling articulately narrated the action we could barely discern, he casually alluded at every turn to the rich history of the game, its traditions, its stars, its strategies.

The arrival of the NHL in Buffalo with the league's second expansion in 1970 afforded us new chances to learn. As the relatively small, if avid and knowledgeable, hockey subculture mushroomed to include latecomers attracted by a major-league glow, newsstands, bookstores, and libraries began to stock books on hockey. A three-eighths-of-an-inch-thin mass-market paperback out of Winnipeg, purchased at a suburban drugstore, was our first hockey encyclopaedia. The school library furnished a copy of one of Brian McFarlane's books of historical anecdotes for young readers. If you went down to the Aud for a Sabres game, a tiny old man with a thick accent stood in the darkness and snow outside the main entrance on Terrace Street, your sole source in the area for that ultimate insider's guide to the game, Ken McKenzie's *Hockey News*. Loblaw's ran a sticker-album promotion; the stickers, the photos of NHL players, were a premium with every *x* dollars you spent on groceries, but while it was satisfying to collect them all, the real joy lay in the brief player biographies on every page, listing the obscure rural Canadian towns from which each player hailed and the junior team for which he'd played. This last artifact, this quaint, weird piece of ephemera, may somehow have had more effect than anything in shaping our view of the game, and possibly our view of the world.

Those sources seem almost laughable now, but they served their purpose as a primer for our education as hockey fans. They gave us a small window onto the world of hockey, onto where the game had come from, where it had been, who had made it what it was. In another city, in a different year, at a different age, with different sources, our initial impression would have been otherwise, and our lasting impression perhaps a different one as well. If we'd been brought up in Toronto, or Atlanta, if it had been the 1930s, or the 1990s, if we'd been adults at the time instead of kids, then maybe, maybe we'd have a different take on where hockey is now, where it's heading and where it ought to go.

But we had the opportunity to see Cournoyer and Keon, to see Plante and Beliveau and Hull, to hear Gallivan and Foster Hewitt, King Clancy and Red Storey, and to learn the game's traditions. And all of hockey's heroic tales—Bobby Baun and his broken ankle, Lester Patrick's stint in the nets, Mud Bruneteau's marathon-ending goal, the Dawson City challenge and One-Eyed Frank McGee... all of the game's tragic figures—Howie Morenz, Charlie Gardiner, Ace Bailey, Bill Barilko, Hobey Baker... all the gentlemen and wildmen, and the wonderfully ridiculous moments—Ted Lindsay, Carl Brewer, Frank Nighbor, Frank Frederickson, Newsy Lalonde, Sprague Cleghorn, even the Cup itself, on the curb and as a flowerpot and drop-kicked into the Rideau Canal... all the great stories and all the great characters, a thousand and one nights of hockey heroism and tragedy and humour, soon became known to us and evoked for us all the romance of the game.

When you or your kids, or we or our kids, pull on parkas and tramp through the snow, carrying shovels and sticks out to the frozen pond in the farm field or the city park or the suburban backyard, and lace up the skates with frozen fingers and play till we can't feel our feet anymore, we're all seeing and feeling exactly what so many who love hockey, from you and us and childhood pals to the best the game has ever known, have seen and felt for generations. And the greats are out there with us; out on the pond, you're Maurice Richard breaking in on Turk Broda, or we're Roger Crozier trying to stop Phil Esposito, and in their own minds the kids are Paul Kariya and Brian Leetch and Patrick Roy.

All of that now stands in jeopardy. This is the NHL today; this is hockey as we enter the 21st century—nondescript teams with nondescript personnel playing in nondescript converted basketball arenas, where fans must have offside and icing explained to them constantly as club employees in oversized mascot costumes cavort desperately in half-empty stands trying to whip up enthusiasm, while down below players toddle about in ridiculous uniforms depicting suns and palm trees, crudely drawn carnivores baring claws, talons, fangs, and other emblems of flesh-rending ferocity. Even back in the cities where people know hockey, fans now sit three city blocks away from the ice to watch faceless teams play in enormous, sterile new arenas, buildings with the ambience of an aircraft hangar, which have replaced hockey's quirky, tradition-rich ancient cathedrals and the fond memories they held. And on the ice itself, what once was the fastest team sport on earth has now been reduced to a dreary shuffle by tedious clutch-and-grab tactics, outlandishly oversized equipment, obtrusive technology, inconsistent officiating, idiotic rule changes, and an endless schedule of meaningless games. All the history and the magic of the game, all the best things about hockey, all the things that make it special, are being tossed aside and ploughed under in a greed-driven frenzy of breakneck overexpansion, shopping-mall arenas, garish merchandising and glitzy promotions, ludicrous rule proposals and lacklustre play.

Hockey today is inarguably at a crossroads. But it has arrived there having lost its compass. It would be easy enough to regain its bearings by taking a hard look back at the long path it has taken for a century and a quarter, since the very beginning of its journey in Victorian Canada. The path ahead would become clear. To ignore it—to avoid it and veer off in another direction—would be a dangerous mistake. If this is the way hockey is going, its gaze transfixed by the mirage of some distant Eldorado of untold profit, straying from the trail it has taken through all the years from a mist-shrouded, frozen pond somewhere between Montreal and Kingston and Halifax, what will the game become? There must be a desire to have the game's history not merely enshrined in some museum like a religious relic or a shard of pottery from an extinct civilization, but to have it sustained as a living thing, to keep all the hockey that's still to be played relevant to all that's gone before—to make the game as it was played by Gretzky and Richard and Vezina, and all the great stars and all the obscure role players who've performed over the decades, manifest in the game that's played tonight, and this season, and in all the years to come.

Chapter 2

more is less

We can only hope that even if the people running the NHL don't recognize the problems hockey faces, they can at least recognize sarcasm. But if the subtle barbs of the quick-witted intermission host of "Hockey Night in Canada" don't register with them, we're here to swing the sledgehammers. Because we're running out of patience with them. The season *does* drag on forever. Yet how many positive memories did the 1997-98 season provide? Any monumental clashes or unforgettable moments there for you amid all those teams and all those games? No, not for us either, really. An endless, uneventful, pale grey blur of meaningless games, a goal-scoring drought spreading from Ottawa to Vancouver to San Jose and across the hot alien landscape of the American southland to Anaheim to Phoenix to Dallas to Miami to Raleigh or Durham or Greensboro or someplace, games without differentiation or drama, without emotion or impact.

What does it say when there are empty seats at virtually every game in Boston and Montreal's cavernous new buildings? Isn't it obvious? Don't the NHL owners and Gary Bettman, their commissioner, get it? For the fans, every aspect of the hockey experience is becoming a cheap, shabby counterfeit of what made the game great. And it's the NHL's predilection for wretched excess that's responsible.

If the prospect of any one game—played at some atrocity of a modern arena between two teams half of whose rosters are minor-league-quality players, all wearing hideous roller-hockey-style uniforms, playing ultra-cautious clutch-and-grab hockey that may or may not produce a couple of goals the whole night—isn't bad enough, try more than a thousand such games, starting as summer is just beginning to wane, and churning on endlessly until the trees are back in bloom and the jackets are back in the closet. And then continuing on through the playoffs, where almost a hundred more games sprawl across spring and on into summer, with the Stanley Cup still being contested as you prepare for your Canada Day barbecue.

It reminds us of the time we ordered burgers and fries at a little greasy-spoon diner. The fries arrived overdone—every one of them burnt—but there was a mountain of them. "Sorry about the fries," said the waitress, snapping her chewing gum, "but I brought you extra to make up for it."

Well, no tip for you, honey. Quantity is no substitute for quality. Twenty-seven teams, let alone thirty, is way too many. Eighty-two games per team is way too many. An NHL schedule of 1,107 games, even if the action was excellent, is simply way, way too long. Maybe it's time for a little history lesson. So many new fans we run into—kids especially, but adult newcomers to the game as well—seem to have the notion that hockey has always been in this state, that all the teams playing now have played throughout its history, that its history, in fact, extends all the way back to the early 1980s. That's due in large part to the NHL marketing itself as some sort of designer sport, like arena football, and to hockey's history having been more poorly served and presented by the NHL than any other sport's has been by its own premier league.

The roller coaster profile opposite charts the average number of goals scored per game in each season of the NHL's existence. We've left out the figures from the NHL's predecessors and rivals—the International Pro League, the Eastern Canada Hockey Association, the National Hockey Association, the Pacific Coast Hockey Association, the Western Hockey League, all from the first quarter of this century, and the World Hockey Association of the 1970s—but we'll mention them here just for the benefit of all those new fans who think it was the NHL that invented hockey and not the other way around.

It's useful to put the scoring averages in some context. The NHL began with four teams playing 22-game schedules. By the late 1920s, the league had ten teams playing 44 games each; the entire NHL slate comprised 220 games. The 18 years of the Original Six era featured a stable 70-game schedule—a 210-game season. Even after the NHL doubled in

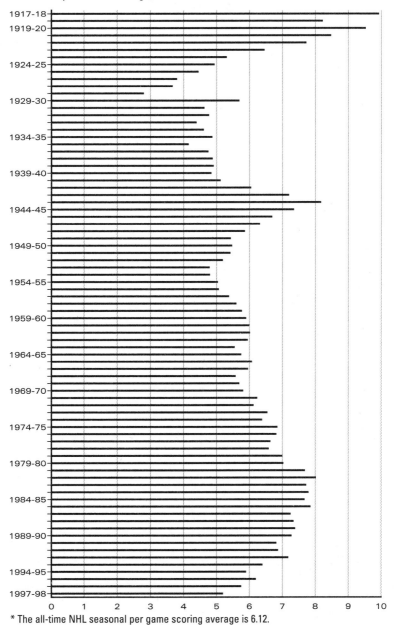

NHL Goals per Game Average, 1917-18 - 1997-98*

* The all-time NHL seasonal per game scoring average is 6.12.

size with the 1967 expansion, there were less than half as many games in the season as there are now—444 that first expansion year, 456 the next two, 546 in the early '70s. Within a decade, the NHL slate has gone from 840 games in 1990-91, to 880 in '91-92, to 1,008 in '92-93, to 1,066 in '95-96, and by 2000-01, once the league has finished tacking on four more expansion franchises, it'll take an appalling 1,230 games to complete the season. At which point, presumably, in order to get all the games in, non-playoff clubs will have to start playing their regular-season schedules while the rest of the teams are still participating in the previous season's playoffs.

It's all about money, of course, and if you want to be as cynical as the NHL, or any pro sports league, or any multibillion-dollar international corporation, you can say, What isn't? Sadly, you'd probably be right. And we're not about to chastise the NHL simply for wanting to make money. Hell, we *all* want to make money. But most of us draw some line at what and whom we exploit in order to do that. The NHL's lust for the lucre of expansion fees—not to mention the prices it dares to charge fans for tickets—smacks of shamelessness. It's exploiting the fans by pricing the game out of their reach, and it's exploiting the game itself by degrading the level of play. The ironic thing is that this craven money grab, in and of itself, is turning away the very fans the NHL claims to want and need, and the results of this naked greed—the severe damage it's done to the quality of the NHL's on-ice product—have even further disenchanted hockey's existing fan base.

The concept of "less is more" is apparently alien thinking to the NHL. We won't start here on what a disaster the interminable schedule is in terms of marketing strategy. Just on an aesthetic basis alone, can't Bettman and the lords of the NHL see what every fan sees as teams go through the motions in meaningless regular-season games? Why should players be expected to exert themselves to the limit night after night after night, leaving them exhausted or injured at playoff time, when a .500 record will get their team into post-season play? Why should we fans be expected to pay $20, or $50, or $100 or more for a seat, or thousands of dollars for season tickets, to see our team give a half-hearted effort against some equally unenthusiastic Sun Belt team we couldn't care less about?

One reason the National Football League is so far ahead of the NHL in both profit and prestige is the brevity of its schedule. Another is the familiarity of the opposition. Each team plays just 16 games, and every year half of those are against the same division rivals. Every game is huge—an event, a war, that spells the difference between making the playoffs or being left out. A team takes just one Sunday afternoon off, and come January they'll be looking back at it as the reason they're on the road for the playoffs or at home cleaning out the garage. The frequency of division play builds rivalries and grudges that make the Balkans look like a pillow fight—Packers and Vikings, Bills and Dolphins, Cowboys and Redskins, Chiefs and Raiders—those teams *hate* each other, and their *fans* hate each other. It's glorious. Is the Canadiens-Bruins rivalry a shadow of what it once was? Do the Leafs and the Red Wings remember that they even *had* a rivalry? These teams used to play each other 14 times a year! Now they're just another couple of nights on the schedule amid a mind-numbing grind of seven months and 82 games.

We're hardly suggesting the NHL return to the schedule it played in its early years, but imagine the intensity of every game in those days. The Eastern Canada Hockey Association and the National Hockey Association, the linear antecedents of the NHL, started with 12-game seasons in 1909 and 1910. The Pacific Coast Hockey Association, the NHA's major rival, began with a 16-game slate. The NHL schedule was 22 games in its 1917-18 maiden season, 18 in its second year, and 24 for the next five campaigns. Any brief slump was enough to ruin a team's whole season, and the players knew it. Every game meant something. Every game counted. NHL teams played seasons ranging from 44 to 50 games between 1926-27 and 1945-46. Bearing that in mind, think back just a couple of years to the lockout-shortened 1994-95 NHL season. Once the players shook off a few months' worth of rust and began to realize how much was on the line every night, didn't that 48-game season produce some of the most intense, desperate, hard-fought, regular-season action, game for game and night by night, you've seen in years?

The sheer enormousness of the 82-game season is one of the most dismal things about hockey today. What real meaning is there in any one game with so many to be played? There's no feeling that there's anything really at stake on any given night until the final week or two of the season, when contending clubs might find a reason to battle for the dubious advantage of a single extra game at home in the playoffs, and a few stragglers try to avoid missing the playoff cut entirely just so they can be knocked out in the opening round.

And even then, does anybody care anymore, unless their team is in the playoff mix? Not according to Detroit's Scotty Bowman, whose name will soon have to be legally changed to Scotty Bowman-the-winningest-coach-in-NHL-history. "When you're involved like us," Bowman said during the 1998 Cup Final, "the season is never too long. But I imagine for a lot of other people they've had enough of it. You do start in October. This deep into the playoffs, it seems the interest is heavy in only the cities that it's played in. I don't know how much interest there is around the rest of the league. I don't even know in places like Montreal or Toronto, cities that have a long hockey heritage, how much interest there even is there."

Nor did Bowman hold out much hope for improvement. "They're not going to shorten the schedule. It probably won't happen in my time. They'll probably increase it."

The NHL went to a 70-game schedule in 1949-50, which was probably a lot more than could be justified for a six-team circuit, but hey, owners were greedy louts then, too. The benefit for the fans, though, was how often the teams played each other. Aficionados of the Original Six era still wax poetic over the intensity of the rivalries in those years. Somehow we can't imagine Blackhawks fans getting quite that worked up over the Atlanta Thrashers or Columbus Blue Jackets.

The fact is, we're paying NHL prices to watch IHL teams. Let's look at 1966 again. Six teams with 17-man rosters. One hundred and two NHL players. How many guys today could make one of those teams? Not because "today's player isn't half the player we had in those days" or any of that claptrap; we're of the firm conviction that the best players of today, or the Original Six era, or from the dawn of the NHL, would have been among the best players in any era you could set them down in.

No, the point is that only the best hundred players of the Original Six had the opportunity to compete in the NHL. You can begin to under-stand why fans who grew up watching the game in those days still get misty-eyed over the level of play they saw. Take a few minutes sometime and pick the six best goaltenders, the 35 best defencemen, and the top 60 or 70 forwards in the NHL today, divide them into six rosters, and imag-ine the quality of the games you'd see them play against one another.

Still and all, the claustrophobically insular six-team era was actually bad for hockey in many ways, and one of those ways was that lots of guys with major-league ability were consigned to a life in the minors. Expansion, at that point, was a great thing, even in the one fell swoop of 1967, because, as would quickly be proven by the success of many of those teams and many of the players who finally got their chance in the NHL, there was indeed enough talent available to supply 12 major-league teams.

There was, in fact, talent enough for yet a couple more, but not nearly enough to cope with the runaway expansion sparked by the NHL's war of one-upmanship with the WHA. The 12 new WHA fran-chises created in 1972 grabbed dozens of players of every level of ability from the NHL and scoured the minors for whatever the NHL hadn't already used to plug the holes. The NHL, seriously concerned about the WHA's not inconsiderable star power and the rebel circuit's growth into a legitimate rival, began cooking up expansion franchises like the car-nival makes corn dogs, not because there was a demand for new teams, not because hockey was ready for more teams, but simply in a pre-emptive effort to put teams in cities before the WHA could.

By 1974-75, major-league hockey included a staggering 32 teams in two leagues. While the play of a few top teams remained brilliant, much of the hockey of the mid- to late-'70s was hilarious in its ineptitude. With the well of talent sucked completely dry, NHL expansion teams like the Islanders, Capitals, and Scouts set all-time records for futility, and empty seats were the order of the day in hastily recruited American outposts like Oakland, Kansas City, Denver, Atlanta and Cleveland. It was a mess—kind of like the NHL today. First-division clubs routinely ran up double-digit scores against second-division sides. In a desperate scramble to obtain any warm body that could skate, the WHA turned to Europe for players. It found a few great ones. It also found a lot who were no better than third-liners, but conditions being what they were, those guys got to play too. Still, they added a couple of inches to the talent pool, and when the WHA finally gave up the ghost in 1979, the NHL stood as the sole major league and with a somewhat more manageable total of 21 teams.

The 1980s ushered in the Age of Air Hockey, which demonstrated that the league-wide level of talent was still uncomfortably low. Defence, weakened by expansion and degraded by the advent of clutch-and-grab, found itself woefully overmatched by the arrival of European-style offence in the late 1970s and 1980s. Teams now ran up double-digit scores, not only against cellar-dwelling sides, but regularly came close to doing it against each other in the same game. Every night, games wound up 8-5, 10-6, 12-7, in a nauseating parade of goals, goals, goals, goals, goals, goals, goals—the tenfold tabulation of the goals! It wasn't just the boy wonder Gretzky, it wasn't just the Oilers; every year it seemed like half a dozen teenagers and unheralded minor leaguers, several of whom would go on to journeyman careers, just walked right into the league and banged out 40-goal seasons. With scoring inflation devaluing the goal like the Weimar Deutschmark, every team in the NHL set club records for offence during those years. When you scanned the sports page for last night's scores, you had to double-check to make sure you were reading the hockey summaries and not the results from team handball.

But fortunately for the game, the NHL remained stable at 21 teams, and by the late '80s the goal-scoring fever had finally broken. Defence began to re-emerge and reassert itself as coaches adapted and players developed. Another factor was an even larger influx of the best players not only from Europe but from the old Soviet Union as well. With the level of talent almost replenished, with the number of franchises again stable, offence and defence once again approached the precarious equilibrium that makes for hockey at its best.

And then, just as order was finally restored, just as hockey was more healthy than it had been in years, just as the game was actually fun once more, the nightmare began anew. In came the San Jose Sharks. In came Tampa Bay and Ottawa. The North Stars were ripped out of Minnesota and moved to Dallas. In came Florida, and the Mighty Ducks of Anaheim. The Nordiques were yanked out of Quebec and packed off to Denver. The Jets were torn away from Winnipeg and planted out in Phoenix. The Whalers were trundled out of Hartford and plopped down somewhere in the Carolinas. New franchises were fabricated for Nashville, Atlanta, Minnesota, and Columbus, Ohio. It was like watching the old cups-and-balls shell game, except that the NHL kept adding more cups and had no balls at all.

Five new teams in three years were more than enough to shatter the fragile balance hockey had been flailing and reeling for 20 years to reacquire. With North America, Europe, and Russia already plumbed for every available NHL-worthy player, expansion, for the first time in history, actually had a suppressing effect on scoring. There were other reasons, as we'll see a little later, but expansion had at last diluted the NHL to utter insubstantiality. The vaporized residue of major-league scoring talent, spread to a thin mist over 26 teams, barely registered as precipitation on NHL goal nets.

NHL teams, every one of which had once been able to boast at least two forward lines of highly capable scorers and a couple of decent-scoring checkers as well, now were lucky to feature just two individual forwards with genuine scoring ability. Think about it. What teams today have any real depth up front? Detroit, Colorado, possibly Philadelphia... you might be able to argue for one or two more, but after that—nada. In fact, our hats are off to you if you can even *name* the second-line forwards for most teams.

Dallas coach Ken Hitchcock registered his consternation at the state of affairs, noting the 1997-98 exhumations of minor-league journeymen like Rob Brown, Tony Hrkac, Brian Bellows, Pavol Demitra, and Terry Yake as NHL teams searched for anyone—*anyone*—who might score goals. "You get a sense of how desperate teams are for offence," said Hitchcock.

By 2000, that dissipated haze of offence will be scattered among

30 teams. *Thirty teams.* Be afraid. Be very afraid. And don't give us any of that junk about how Europe and Russia make the pool of talent so rich. All the best players from Europe and Russia are already here. There's nothing left over there. Even Central Army, the once-mighty pride of Soviet hockey, has been used as a farm team for Pittsburgh, skating around with little Penguins on their sweaters in the wreckage of a Soviet Elite League that's now scarcely better than a recreational association.

"There simply are not enough quality players around to adequately stock four new teams in such short order," writes Jim Kernaghan of the *London Free Press.* "Of all the major North American professional leagues, the one least prepared for growth is the one that's growing fastest."

Kernaghan dug out some numbers for comparison:

> The National Basketball Association office, for example, was proud to report that there are 33,281,000 players at all levels in the United States. Baseball boasts similar numbers. Any given year throughout all American universities and colleges, the cream of thousands of football players come available for the National Football League.
>
> Hockey? There are fewer than half a million players in Canada at levels down to novice, three-quarters of a million in Russia and the number tails off to tens of thousands in the United States and other hockey-playing nations. All told, there aren't two million hockey players of all ages worldwide.

How precisely accurate those numbers are is open to some debate. But if it really does take 33 million participants—and that's just in the

United States; remember, basketball is played around the world—to produce 330 NBA players, that's one out of 100,000 with major-league talent. If it takes 25 million participants to produce 750 major-league players in baseball (and judging by the level of play these days, many of those are minor-leaguers in major-league uniforms), that's one out of 33,000 with big-league ability. With well under two million people playing hockey, from mites and atoms to rec leagues to the pros, that works out generously to requiring that one out of every 3,000 perform at an NHL level.

Even if the desperately optimistic assumption that expansion into the American Sun Belt will magically inspire millions of kids across the southlands to suddenly start playing hockey pans out, and produces thousands of young men with NHL skills, do you really want to spend the next 20 years or more watching bad hockey while you await the arrival of this promised new wave of talent?

The Sun Belt, hockey's mythical promised land. Right. Let's consider hockey's new address. Just five years ago, eight of the 24 teams—one-third of the league—competing in the NHL were based in Canada. That was in 1993, the year Bettman took office. As we write this five years later, in a league three franchises larger, there are two fewer Canadian teams. In two more years, we'll be lucky if the six remaining Canadian teams are still in place, making up one-fifth of a 30-city, 21st-century NHL that's based in places like Miami and Dallas and Nashville and Atlanta. Hockey can't support 30 teams, as we've demonstrated, so even in the most practical terms a league spread that wide and that thin is horrible enough. But what's really unconscionable by every aesthetic and moral standard is tearing the game out by its northern roots and transplanting it into the American Sun Belt, where people wouldn't know King Clancy from Queen Latifah. It's not just Canada, either, not just Winnipeg and Quebec that lost their teams, as terrible as that was. While Edmonton, too, is now threatened annually, monthly even, with relocation, faithful fans in smaller cities in the northern United States also know the fear and pain of having their team taken from them. Hockey-crazed Minnesotans had their team kidnapped by the North Stars' carpetbagging owner, Norm Green, and plunked down in Texas; Hartford's solid little core of fans watched their franchise, once a WHA power, turned into a perennial bad joke and finally spirited off to a witness-protection program somewhere in the Carolinas; Buffalo survived the prospect of losing the Sabres, at least for another couple of years, only by building a new multimillion-dollar arena.

Canadian fans may rail at the departure of their country's NHL franchises to the States and make it an issue of national identity, but for the fans who loved the North Stars and the Whalers, just like the fans who fumed and grumbled in Quebec and raged and wept in Winnipeg, the most immediate and inescapable result is just the same—regardless of where their team went, it's not theirs anymore.

There is a difference, though, which we recognize and wouldn't for a second dismiss. Most American hockey fans do sympathize; most of them think putting expansion teams, let alone relocating Canadian teams, in the Sun Belt is a genuinely stupid and offensive idea. Those fans who can't understand the fuss are mostly not fans at all; they're

mainly bandwagon-hopping neophytes in the cities that have just gotten or are about to get an NHL franchise, who would be just as excited
about getting an NBA team, or a roller hockey team, or an indoor soccer team. They might get a clearer picture of how all Canadians feel at
the loss of any Canadian city's franchise to some metropolis in the
States, if they heard that the Mitsubishi Corporation had just bought
the Chicago Bears and was moving them to Tokyo, or that Silvio
Berlusconi had just bought the Atlanta Braves and was relocating them
to Milan. Try that one out on the next gloating, inbred huckleberry who
gets a letter into *The Hockey News* or posts a message on the Internet
saying something as imbecilic as "Get used to it, Canada! Yee ha! The
NHL is headin' south!"

Well, it sure as hell is, although not in the way it was meant by the
yokel who posted that actual message on the America Online
Grandstand board in the spring of 1998. How galling, how nauseating,
must it have been for Quebec fans to have their Nordiques, champions
in the WHA reduced to cellar dwellers in the NHL, rebuilt and ready
to at last contend for the Stanley Cup, moved, on the brink of glory, to
Denver. Denver, a city where the NHL had already failed; where local
television reporters informed their curious viewers by actually asking
players questions like "What do you call those sticks you hit the,
y'know, 'puck' with?"; where ownership, reaching back into the city's
glorious sports history, rechristened the team the Avalanche, reviving
the name of Denver's *old indoor soccer team.*

The game is at best a novelty to the people in so many of these places.
All the celebration in the NHL offices over the first few seasons of

sellout crowds in Tampa and playoff success in Miami have gone strangely silent, now that the new-car smell of the Panthers and Lightning has been overcome by the gassy stench of how bad those teams have proven to be and how so many fans around the league couldn't care less about them. The arrival of the Whalers in Carolina— disguised, with a metaphorical paper bag over their heads, as the Hurricanes—didn't excite the slightest interest there even at the start. What better than Carolina symbolizes the stupidity of the NHL's idea that some Manifest Destiny is to be found in the Sun Belt? Behold the scene of desolation, feel the sense of emptiness that prevails at a Carolina home game, where the sounds of skating and shooting might be interrupted only by the lonely barking of a redbone hound some-where off in the humid southern night.

Does the NHL really have a grand vision of hockey conquering the continent, coming from a thousand miles behind to flash past auto rac-ing, overtake baseball, surpass football, eclipse basketball, as the great sport of America? Or is it, do ya think, really about the US$50 million the NHL charged San Jose for admission to the league, and the US$50 million it took in from each of Tampa Bay and Ottawa? *Cha-ching!* Or another US$50 million that the NHL owners were able to divide among themselves from each of Anaheim and Florida, not to mention the potential marketing dollars the NHL could smell by letting the Disney Corporation and Blockbuster Video into the club? *Cha-ching!* Or maybe the 80 million bucks the owners will pocket from Nashville, and again in 1999 from Atlanta and Ted Turner, and again in the year 2000 from both Columbus and Minnesota? *Cha-ching! Cha-ching!*

Expansion into the Sun Belt isn't a bad thing in and of itself. It's a good idea to spread the game to new places, to open it up to new influences and break it out of the infertile insularity in which it wallowed for too long. And it's certainly a good idea to try to make it grow in the U.S., both as a participatory sport and as a spectator sport with a greater potential for making money in that nation's big cities and sprawling television markets. Indeed, there have been some success stories in the '90s expansions. Who would have thought that the people of San Jose would embrace their team so enthusiastically, selling out their rink whether their team was pluckily upsetting Detroit in the playoffs or stinking out the joint as a cellar-dweller? Who had ever seen such an ethnically and racially diverse crowd at an NHL game? Miami fans took to the Panthers quickly and entirely unexpectedly. Their plastic-rat barrages were a pleasure to watch no matter how long they held up games because they were one of the few truly fan-generated outbursts of creative enthusiasm in a major sport this continent has seen in a long time. And the Panthers' Spanish-language radio broadcasts are just the kind of thing the rest of the NHL must do, and has completely neglected to do, if it is to grow and prosper in the U.S.

No, it isn't the Sun Belt itself or the presence of hockey there that is wrong—it's the uprooting and transplantation of northern teams into the Sun Belt that is wrong. It's the haphazard, breakneck fashion in which franchise after franchise is minted and dumped into any old southern zip code with a new arena and parking lot, whether or not there are people there who really want hockey, that is wrong. It's the subversion and erasure of the game's culture and traditions in an attempt to "sell" the game to its new audiences that is wrong. And all these wrong reasons for expansion point out what the real reason for expansion is: the king's ransom that NHL teams divvy up with every new franchise the league approves. It only goes to show how little vision and imagination the league really has. Facing rising player salaries and lacking the monster television contracts that baseball, football, and basketball enjoy (even the NHL's new US$600 million contract is but a fraction of these), the league's only idea for increasing its revenue is to screw the fans by raising ticket prices and introducing PSLs—personal seat licences—and watering down the game by whipping up new NHL franchises faster than McDonald's puts up new restaurants.

And with that expansion income fattening the owners' wallets, and with Commissioner Bettman insisting that attendance is still strong and the NHL healthy, the owners still plead poverty to justify mugging the cities their teams play in for new, even bigger, even more modern arenas with even more luxury boxes, for more tax breaks, for bigger cuts of ever inflating parking and concession revenues, and by waving the atrocity of PSLs in the fans' faces. The team lost $3 million last year, whines one, and we're $12 million in the red, cries another, and unless we raise ticket prices even higher and unless we get some help from the city, the state, the province, the federal government, the team is going to have to move to this other city where they'll build us a new arena and let us keep all the arena revenue and fans will consider it a privilege to pay for PSLs.

If owning a team is so hard, if it's really such a lethal, money-losing venture, why, then, are individual multimillionaires and billion-dollar corporations, who presumably know something about how to run a business and how to recognize a bad risk from a good opportunity, lined up around the block to get a major-league franchise in any sport? Is someone, perhaps, possibly, being something less than honest with us?

Who can say for sure? Just how much money's actually coming in and going out is anybody's guess; the financial books of NHL teams are a better-kept secret than the Black Budget of the Pentagon. But here's something you can't dispute: the NFL is the most financially solid entity in North American professional sports, and one where even teams from markets as small as Green Bay and Buffalo are fiscally sound enough that they can afford the kind of players that can get them to the Super Bowl. The two expansion teams the NFL added in 1995 were the first new franchises in almost 20 years. Why doesn't the NFL have to crank out new teams every season? The league's mammoth contracts with three separate American television networks are one huge reason, and one huge reason it has those contracts is the stability the NFL has in the first place, thanks to its brilliant revenue-sharing policy. Big market teams basically share gate and television revenue equally with small market teams; owners were made to realize that what was best for the league and best for the sport was, in the long run, what was best for the individual teams. NFL commissioner Pete Rozelle hammered out that agreement between NFL clubs back in 1963, and it's been a cornerstone of that league's success.

Let's think back now to early 1993 and the investiture of NHL commissioner Bettman. What were the three ideas the architect of the NBA salary cap had for hockey as he took office? Let's see, there was that silly business about replacing the league crest, the very symbol of the NHL… and some hideous joke of an idea about bringing shootouts to NHL games… and oh yeah! The one high-concept, big idea, the one genuinely good idea he had, looking at the plight of the NHL's small-market franchises—revenue sharing! Say—whatever happened to that? Have you heard those words mentioned even once again since he got the job? The owners tapped Bettman as the salary savant who would put a lid on the upward spiral of player salaries; they even locked out the players in 1994-95, throwing away hockey's best-ever chance to grab the brass ring, in order to try to wrestle a salary cap onto the Players Association. It didn't work. Television revenues and the goodwill of the fans were frittered away and half the season went down the tubes without getting a cap in place, let alone any further discussion of a revenue-sharing plan. So player salaries continued to skyrocket, and smaller cities in Canada and the northern United States watched their teams move south. Rather than get its own house in order with an equitable, overarching fiscal plan that might put the Edmontons of the league on an equal financial footing with Chicago and Philadelphia and Dallas, Bettman and the NHL simply resorted to cranking out expansion franchises in order to snatch up the millions of dollars any city with ready cash waved under their noses.

All these teams, all those games, and it's plain that the NHL's motto is Bigger Is Better. Apparently, that is, until it comes to the big picture.

Chapter 3

flat on the ice

In Calgary, a 21-year-old student visiting from England streaked naked across the ice during a recent game between the Flames and Florida Panthers. Julian Vaudrey, who was arrested and charged with indecency and causing a disturbance, fled Canada two days later. He forfeited $100 bail and could be arrested if he returns to the country. Vaudrey said he made the naked dash because he was bored.

—Bloomberg News Service, January 16, 1998

"I talk to a lot of friends around the league and they say watching the National Hockey League isn't as much fun anymore," says Phoenix forward Jeremy Roenick. "It's boring hockey. That stupid trap system—whoever invented it should be shot. It's the stupidest friggin' hockey ever."

Roenick is right: hockey *has* become boring. The catastrophic drop in league-wide scoring is the game's most widely recognized problem, but it's only one aspect of far more deep-seated troubles involving so much more than can be explained by catchphrases like "the neutral-zone trap."

Absurdly bloated goaltending equipment straight out of the costume shop for *The Road Warrior*; the enlarged goal crease instituted to protect netminders from the interference from which the rulebook already provided protection; interminable video-replay decisions in nearly every game, robbing all goalscoring of the dramatic, explosive, almost sexual release it had provided for a hundred years; obstruction, interference, hooking, and outright tackling up and down the ice, unpenalized as NHL officials refuse—or have been directed by league executives to refuse—to call the game by the book.... The result of all this has been disastrous. In the 1992-93 season the average NHL game featured 7.2 goals and 62 shots; only five years later, it averages little more than just 5.2 goals and fewer than 54 shots. There are days when more goals are scored in soccer's English Premier League than in a full slate of NHL games.

Hockey knows it's in trouble in this department. "Where have all the goals gone?" It's the topic of cover stories in *The Hockey News*; hardly a weekly issue came out during the 1997-98 season without a feature, a column, and half the letters page devoted to the topic. It's the substance of feature articles in *Sports Illustrated*, which traditionally has paid as much attention to hockey as it has to water polo. Flyers owner Ed Snider went on record at the NHL's winter meetings in January 1998 equating low scoring with low attendance. As we write this, it's the main problem baffling the brain trust known as the NHL Rules Committee.

Anyone who's tuned in to a hockey broadcast has heard the stats rolled out (and if you haven't, you can look at the chart on page 15): 1997-98, 5.20 goals per game, the lowest figure since 1955-56.

The 1997-98 season saw a whopping 160 shutouts, far and away the most ever; only two teams, the Rangers and Calgary, failed to get one, while every other NHL team posted at least three. Just five years earlier, the entire NHL schedule produced just 69. The '97-98 season spawned six scoreless games, the most in 62 years.

The balance between offence and defence is an absolutely critical one—its fulcrum the point at which anticipation and intention meet accident and surprise, with the boredom of numbing excess on one side and the boredom of frustrating insufficiency on the other. It's the very essence of the drama of competition, the sexual tension between denial and release.

If the NHL of the 1980s lived through an orgy of goal scoring that was pornographic in its volume and repetition, the NHL of the last few years, by contrast, just ain't gettin' any. Like the loser at the singles club who knows before he even makes his move that he's going to be rejected, the decisive moment of a great scoring chance no longer provoked the exhilarating doubt as to whether the result would be a score or a great save; it was always a save. And often not even a great one. Just routine, or at least they seemed routine, because you'd come to expect them. And on they went into overtime, one after another.

Nowhere is the tediousness of play more evident than in what should be the NHL's showcase—the playoffs and their all-too-frequent resort to overtime. There was a time, not so long ago, when a Stanley Cup game that went into overtime was a reason to wake the kids and call the neighbours. It was an event not to be missed, a tension-fraught, sweat-drenched, adrenalin-pumping crystallization of the best that hockey had to offer. Two of the game's better teams, playing smart, tough, desperate hockey; players racing and battling for every loose puck while ever-mindful of their position, striving to create the one chance that could win it all, aware that any mistake, any overcommitment, any miscue, any lack of attention to detail could finish their team—it was an electrifying five or ten or maybe fifteen minutes, and then in an explosive flash of ecstasy or horror it was over. If the goaltending was downright heroic, and it went to a second overtime—and a game or two would go that far every two or three years—it was cause to go to the medicine cabinet at intermission and gulp down some digitalis. And if they actually extended that into a third OT, my God, it was unbelievable, it was something you saw only a few times in your life, something you talked about for years.

We can still picture Jim Pappin's second-OT winner for Chicago in the 1971 Final, the second-OT goal Cam Connor scored for the Habs against Toronto in the '79 quarterfinals, Pat LaFontaine's spinnerama slapper that decided the four-OT Easter Epic for the Isles in 1987; we remember where we were when we saw them and everything about that night. And they weren't spectacular highlight-reel goals; they didn't even involve our team. Unless you're a fan of one of the sides involved, do you really recall much about any of the goals that brought a merciful end to any of the marathon OT sessions in the last several years, or anything, really, about those games at all?

The old pre-overtime pastime—picking the guy from each team you predict will score the winner—has been replaced by a new question in the last few seasons. Now it's "How many OTs do you think it will take?"—every playoff year, any number of games hit a second overtime, a third overtime, a fourth, with teams playing soft baseline lobs from one blue line to the other until two in the morning and producing new cures for insomnia. The rarity has become the commonplace, something not to be marvelled at, but to be dreaded, not something that rivets your attention but something that makes you roll your eyes.

In the 21 post-seasons from 1968 to 1988, there were 1,150 playoff games; 17 (1.5%) reached a second overtime or beyond. In the ten years that followed, there were 846 playoff games; 41 (4.8%) required a second overtime or beyond. In the 26 post-seasons from 1968 to 1993, just two of 1,578 playoff games (0.1%) saw a third overtime period; in the three post-seasons from 1996 through 1998, five out of 247 playoff games (2.0%) have seen a third overtime or beyond.

In the current offence-suppressing atmosphere, these sorts of results are inevitable. But if the NHL is serious about wanting the game to be appealing on TV, and if it cares about its network contracts, multiple overtimes are about the last thing it should want to see, because they are awful as far as TV is concerned. The networks hate all these unpredictably extended sessions. They want their programming in prescribed blocks, so the game doesn't push back or cut into more highly rated, scheduled shows. And the NHL should want the games to finish before viewers either nod off or just turn off the game to go to bed.

If hockey won't learn its lessons from sports that have used television well to promote themselves, can it at least learn what not to do from those that used television badly? Like baseball, which spent decades chasing prime-time advertising dollars, but disaffected an entire generation by broadcasting its premier events—the World Series and the All-Star Game—so late at night that kids across most of the continent were in bed by the third inning. Now those kids are adults, who play basketball and watch football and don't give a hoot about baseball. Just like their own kids. And now it's hockey's premier event—the Stanley Cup playoffs—winding on into the wee hours as fans wait in vain for somebody to remember how to score. You tell us what hockey is today: the fastest, most exciting sport on earth? Or a dull, low-scoring game that few Americans play or even watch.

If it's vital to hockey's health that the game succeed in the States, if it's crucial to make the game popular in the U.S., isn't it vital that the game be a good one, that play be of a high calibre? Don't you have to ensure that there is excitement? Like, maybe goals, for instance? Soccer is the most popular sport on earth, but it is struggling as major-league entertainment in Canada and the United States for two main reasons: first, North American sports fans' refusal to embrace a "foreign" game, particularly one in which the best players are not home-grown; and second, in spite of the NASL's and MLS's presence as very wide-open, free-scoring affairs by soccer standards, North Americans' unshakeable perception of soccer as a dull, low-scoring game.

So we come down to the question that obsesses the hockey media and confounds the NHL itself—what happened to the offence? Where are the goals? Everybody has a pet theory. *It's that stupid neutral-zone trap! Or, the goaltenders are so much better today! Or, the stupid refs never call a penalty! Or, the stupid refs call way too many penalties! Or, it's because Fox's glowing puck bounces too much!* Or, *all those lousy European players are taking jobs away from Canadians who can score!* Or, *it's all because of El Niño!*

Just the fact that there *are* so many theories should be your first clue that it's no one single thing. When you see a radical shift in the amount of scoring, when there's a sea change in the way a game is played and the results it produces, you can be sure there's a combination of forces at work. Like when scoring mushroomed in the 1980s—it wasn't just the debasement of defence through expansion and the toleration of clutch-and-grab, it wasn't just the adaptation of the criss-crossing, cycling style of EuroSoviet offensive strategies: it was those two things in tandem, each magnifying the effect of the other. So grab your binoculars, your magnifying glass, your field guides and specimen jars and your notebook, and throw on your safari jacket and pith helmet. We're going on a little field trip to see just what's wreaking havoc on hockey's ecosystem.

We've already looked at the decimating effect that expansion has had and will continue to have; we've examined the dulling influence of the insanely protracted schedule. Jot those down in your journals; they're important factors. But there's more at work here. Those things were already present to some extent five years ago, and the game was still great then. Into the duck blind, everyone—we shall observe the neutral-zone trap in its native habitat.

A lot of fans regard the trap with suspicion and disgust, as some sort of gimmicky, unsporting dirty trick, cruel and artificial, as if a giant blade suspended from the rafters swung back and forth across the trapping team's blue line. This is what happens when one guy shouts and nobody else thinks. The trap becomes a buzzword, and people in the sports media who wouldn't know the neutral zone from "The Twilight Zone" start pontificating about how the trap is ruining the game. Its tactical cousin, the left-wing lock, gets about as much respect. But the coaches love it. Why? Because it works. There's no denying that. So why should we or you hate it? Because you want your team to play poorly on defence and give up a lot of goals? Of course not. Because it's some newfangled strategy that's ruining the game? Of course not. The trap, by whatever name, is nothing new.

Legendary Dartmouth coach Eddie Jeremiah detailed something very like the trap—referring to it as the "wing backcheck"—in his 1942 classic *Ice Hockey*, and Lloyd Percival suggested something very similar in describing the "counter play" in *The Hockey Handbook*, his famous 1960 tract. The trap and lock strategies were pioneered in the NHL by the Canadiens dynasty of the 1950s and carried on by later Cup-hoarding Hab sides in the late '60s and early '70s. These were the Flying Frenchmen editions of the Habs, fantastic scoring machines, and the trap certainly wasn't their main strategy—but it was in their bag of tricks, useful when protecting a slim lead. Where do you think Jacques Lemaire picked it up in the first place?

The trap, the lock—it's not rocket science, and it's not done with mirrors. Without diagramming all the Xs and Os, there's really not all that much more to it than keeping one of your forwards high to influence which side of the ice the team breaking out with the puck will go to, then keeping their wingers to the outside. Isn't that just common sense? Isn't that just good fundamental transition play and defence? Things just got so sloppy and undisciplined in the 1980s, apparently, that everybody forgot about those concepts and failed to recognize them when they reappeared.

The great thing about the trap and the lock—that is, if you're playing for or rooting for a team that uses them—is that they limit the ability of an offensively gifted opponent to freewheel and get players open for odd-man breaks. If your team is loaded with speedy forwards and mobile defencemen who can all stickhandle and score, and if you have a good goalie who can stop all the three-on-twos and breakaways the other team will get, you don't need the trap; you'd prefer to play a firewagon style, because you can do it better than the other guys and you'll win most high-scoring, end-to-end games. But in the NHL today, there's hardly a team that's able to play firewagon hockey; thanks to unbridled overexpansion, nobody has more than a handful of players with the level of talent to win with a wide-open, defence-be-damned kind of style.

Certainly the 1991-92 New Jersey Devils didn't. Their leading scorer that season, Claude Lemieux, wound up 50th in the NHL in scoring. But when Lemaire became the Devils' coach the following season, he found he had a lot of guys capable of playing a smart positional game; they promptly bought into his trapping system, and in 1995 the Stanley Cup was being driven in little circles around the Meadowlands parking lot in what passed for a victory parade. We're not giving away any government secrets when we say hockey coaches are quicker to copy somebody else's successful idea than Hong Kong toy manufacturers. The following year, at least half the teams in the NHL employed some version of the trap or the lock at least some of the time, and the three-year-old

Florida Panthers, another team with a great goalie and an army of smart, smallish checkers who couldn't score to save their lives, worked the trap to near-perfection and actually got all the way to the Cup Final.

Nonetheless, they were swept away by talent-rich Colorado, who were led by the extraordinary centremen Sakic and Forsberg. In 1997, Detroit, a team even deeper in talent and skill than the Avalanche, dispatched lumbering, oversized Philadelphia. And the Red Wings kept the Cup in 1998, despite putting out a full effort for only about half of each game in the Final. The most eye-catching episode of the 1998 Cup series against Washington, in fact, was the third period of Game 2, when, confronted with a 3-1 deficit on the scoreboard, Detroit suddenly found its "on" switch, and for the next 30 minutes channelled the spirit of the Canadiens of 1958, or of 1978. They were, of course, the Red Wings of 1998, and that they utterly overwhelmed the Caps with that approach, running up 60 shots and winning 5-4 after 15 minutes of overtime, may be a good omen. The success of talent-heavy clubs like Detroit and Colorado, playing good and often great two-way hockey, should set a new example for imitative coaches and general managers. It's still true, as it has always been, that defence wins championships. You still need goaltending, and defencemen who can clear the front of the net and move the puck out, and forwards who can backcheck. But it's foolish to play defence to the deliberate exclusion of offence when you've got the horses to take the play to the other team. Most clubs will continue to play cautious, defence-first systems because they know they don't have the horses. But a few will overestimate their talent and try to open it up nevertheless, and a few will realize they need top-flight talent and depth if they're really serious about laying their hands on the Cup.

The trap, the lock, and the whole strategic approach that eschews taking any chances to create scoring, in favour of minimizing any possibility of the other team scoring, aren't new, and they aren't evil; they're really the inevitable and unavoidable response to the conditions that prevail in a league grown too vast and diluted for most teams to play any other way. But as we have shown, teams in the past have been successful using defensive systems without causing a league-wide scoring brownout. The trap is a factor, but it isn't the whole story either.

Let's consider something more obvious. If the quality of play has fallen off, maybe it's because the quality of player has fallen off. It's an inarguable fact that an NHL horrifyingly stretched out to 27 clubs, soon to be 30, has left most of its teams with only a couple of star players and is stocked largely with guys who in any other era would have been playing out their careers in the minor leagues. That's a big factor in the scoring drought; make a note of it in your field journals. But let's think even further about the kind of player every team seems to be looking for nowadays.

When you hear about a highly touted junior prospect or read scouting reports on him leading up to the NHL entry draft, do you hear about his stickhandling ability or the accuracy of his backhand shot? You do if it's a lengthy, detailed report; it's somewhere down there in the fine print, like an insurance disclaimer. First and foremost, though, you hear about how huge and strong he is. He's a "big, physical" kid, with "tremendous upper body strength," who's impressed scouts by having "beefed up" and "added 25 pounds of muscle." These, clearly, are good things if you want to be a football lineman. And they're probably worthwhile attributes if you want to be a crease-clearing defenceman. But no matter what position you play, or what style you play, or how much skill you have, if you lack footballian stature and brawn, it's a big red demerit stamped across the top of your scouting report.

How many times have you read something along the lines of "has great skills, but probably too small to compete at NHL level." Size and aggressiveness have always been prized, but ever since Team Canada banged and barged their way to desperate victory in 1972 those qualities seem to have overtaken skill in importance—a fascination accelerated by the subsequent NHL stardom of big, physical players like Rick Tocchet, Kevin Stevens, and Cam Neely, and sealed by the superstardom of Eric Lindros.

Coaches and scouts now heap attention on youth players who develop precocious size, and neglect equally or more skilled smaller players. How many potential professional-level finesse players become too discouraged to pursue a career by the time they hit their teens, and how many youngsters go on to pad out NHL rosters thanks mainly to their size and the encouragement they got because of it, is an open question. But it all seems an extremely odd shift in thinking. One more great thing about hockey has always been that even at the highest levels it's a game played by people of normal human dimensions; you don't need to be bigger and heavier than a walk-in freezer, like in football, or taller than a streetlamp, like in basketball. Conventional wisdom among coaches and scouts, right into the '70s, had always been that the largest players tended to be the least skilled, generally inferior in speed, quickness, stickhandling skills, and so on. And the outstanding success over the last 20 or 25 years of players like Marcel Dionne, Denis Savard, Danny Gare, Dennis Maruk, Doug Jarvis, Ray Ferraro, Neal Broten, Mike Rogers, Terry Ruskowski, Mats Naslund, Hakan Loob, Tony Granato, Tomas Jonsson, Curt Giles, right on up through Pat LaFontaine and the few diminutive skaters still remaining in the NHL—Doug Gilmour, Dino Ciccarelli, Steve Thomas, Pat Verbeek, Mark Recchi, Theo Fleury, Pavel Bure, Ziggy Palffy, not to mention some spindly busher named Gretzky—should have caused the bigger-is-better theory to be dismissed without deliberation. Every one of these players is of normal human dimensions or smaller, every one of them with star-quality skills, playing the game any way you like it—pure-as-the-driven-snow dipsy-doodlers, rip-snorting hackers and bangers, and conscientious checkers all plentiful among their number. But never mind all that—if you're anything under six foot and 200 pounds, you'd darn well better be the next Gretzky if you want to get a second glance from the NHL. So let's log in "excessive size at the expense of skill" as another factor in our search for where the scoring's gone. But the bigger quarry lies just ahead.

Mario Lemieux's retirement in 1997 was the most stunning, damning indictment any league in any sport has ever received. When a great player packs it in while he's still at the top of his game, less because of age, or injuries, or personal problems, but ultimately because the style and quality of play in that league stink, that single act says more about the state of the game than we could in 200 pages or an infinite number of monkeys could in an infinite number of Molson commercials.

Lemieux foreshadowed his early retirement as far back as 1992, when his disgust with the level of play prompted him to call the NHL "a garage league."

"There certainly have to be changes made," he said shortly after winning both the Stanley Cup and the Conn Smythe Trophy for the second straight year. "There's too much stickwork, too much slashing, too much interference, and it has gotten way out of hand. We are trying to sell this product to the public." But the NHL failed to heed him then and ignored his continued criticism even through his final campaign, when he said, "It's to the point where it's not hockey anymore—it's like football on skates."

Lemieux, one of the greatest performers in the history of the game, the man who wouldn't let a degenerative spinal condition or Hodgkin's disease or radiation therapy stop him, finally had more than he could stand in the form of the relentless hooking, holding, hacking, and tackling that routinely reduce what should be a spectacle of speed and skill to a sluggish wrestling and shoving match.

"The best teams win in basketball because the players can run up the court without carrying two guys on their backs," Lemieux said. "Not so in hockey. They grab you whether you have the puck or not." You can't call that sour grapes. Lemieux spoke from a platform he'd built for himself out of six NHL scoring titles, three Hart Trophies, and two Stanley Cups.

In no other game is there such a disparity between the rule book and the reality of play. It's an embarrassment to hockey—or it should be—and it's appalling, utterly shameful, that it's gone on this way for more than 20 years.

It used to be different. It really did. Maybe you can remember, but if you can't, go back and look for yourself. Watch the tapes of games from the 1950s and 1960s. We did, partly for the pure entertainment and partly as a reality check, and they were amazing even to us. It had been so long since we'd seen NHL hockey played by the rules, we'd almost forgotten what it looked like. When Beliveau or Mikita came in on a rush on one of those old highlight films and sidestepped a defenceman in the face-off circle to walk in on goal or dish a perfect pass through the slot, our initial reaction wasn't "What a great move"; it was "Why didn't somebody reach out and yank him down?"

Why didn't somebody slash Beliveau across the knee, shove a stick into his navel, haul him in like a gaffed fish, grab him by the sleeve of his sweater, put him in a bear-hug, wrestle him to the ice and lie on top of him until the puck had been cleared out of the zone? Gee, we dunno—maybe *because it was against the rules?*

Considering who had the puck, doing that might have been the smart move—it would have been, in the language of the game, a "good penalty." The point is, *it would have been a penalty.* Back then, anyway. Today it would just be a "good defensive play."

It would be easy—and fun—to blame the Philadelphia Flyers for this. But the real onus falls on the executives who have run the league itself since the early 1970s. That's when clutch-and-grab, hook-and-hold, sit-on-their-chest-'til-there's-a-whistle play became state of the art. It was the Flyers who introduced it, but it was the league that failed to recognize it or do anything about it.

Hard hitting and rough-and-tumble play have always been a part of hockey, and let's hope they always will be. We love a big board-rattling check and a huge open-ice hit as much as anyone. A rolling hip-check that sends the puck carrier cartwheeling through the air is a thing of rare beauty. No pairs figure skating for us, thanks. But the Flyers of the early 1970s were beyond the pale. These weren't just highly skilled roughnecks ready to respond to tough-guy tactics or a cheap shot from the other team; this wasn't just the occasional dust-up born of emotions running high. No, they were something else entirely, a loathsome band of blackguards whose principal tactic was premeditated ultraviolence. It didn't matter if you wanted to play it clean; before the game was a couple of minutes old, usually during the opening face-off if not during the pre-game skate, some knuckle-dragging Piltdown Man—and they had about a dozen of them, all with moronic nicknames—would sucker-punch your best player and pound him into the ice, igniting the first of several bench-clearing brawls that would grind on through the night. And make no mistake, this garbage was wildly popular on both sides of the border. It spread through the NHL, it spread through the minors, it spread into juniors and midgets and rec leagues, and a lot of fans absolutely loved it. The Flyers were the biggest road draw in the league, because if you liked them, you wanted to see them start a brawl, and if you hated them, you wanted to see the shit kicked out of them. *Slapshot*, although brilliant and hilarious and ostensibly about life in the East Coast League, was no exaggeration. Freakish goons with comic-book monikers—that was hockey in the 1970s, and the game was in very real danger of becoming nothing more than pro wrestling on ice at best, and at worst, felony assault.

Things had gotten so far out of hand by 1976 that several incidents of unrestrained brutality that season actually made their way onto the police blotter. They were singled out as particularly extreme, but they weren't really all that much worse than what had been going on in hockey every single night for two or three years at that point. Detroit fist-yobbo Dan Maloney grabbed already unconscious Leaf Brian Glennie and proceeded to repeatedly dash Glennie's head against the ice, sending him halfway into a coma. Rick Jodzio, a thug with the WHA Calgary Cowboys, sparked a Pier 6 brawl when his blindside assault on Quebec's Marc Tardif left the rebel league's leading scorer with a severe concussion. During the ensuing melee, Jodzio returned to pummel Tardif as Tardif was being carried off on a stretcher. And again in Toronto, a Stanley Cup playoff game between the Leafs and Philadelphia ended up with the Flyers swinging fists and sticks not only at the Toronto players but going into the stands to do the same to the fans.

Criminal charges were brought in each case, and you can forget everything said by the "purists" of the day about spotlight-seeking prosecutors. The headlines those prosecutors generated, by publicly humiliating the NHL and hockey in general, were vital in bringing about an end to the 1970s Reign of Terror.

Although it was reluctant to act, the NHL, to its credit, finally did take steps to reduce the more egregious thuggery—the third-man-in rule, the leaving-the-bench penalty, the instigator rule—but it missed a more insidious problem the Flyers introduced and which spread even further and more quickly. You could compare the new contagion, of bending, stretching, and otherwise flouting the rules of the game, to the Black Death—not an inappropriate analogy whenever you talk about the Philadelphia Flyers. When the Black Death rolled through Europe in the 14th century and wiped out a quarter of the world's population, people thought the disease was being spread by the rats overrunning their medieval cities. The connection they drew was logical: the rats were easy to see, and let's face it, a few million sewer rats are pretty gross. So everybody went around killing rats. By the millions. And it didn't do any good. The rats were the obvious, visible problem, but the plague was being transmitted not so much by the rats themselves as by the disease-carrying fleas that infested the rats—and that, once the rat was dead, simply jumped onto the nearest cat, dog, or peasant, infecting them and continuing to spread the disease.

That's sort of how clutch-and-grab came to infest hockey. Along with the fights and the brawls and the malice aforethought, the Flyers dragged every team down to their level by hooking, holding, and interfering with their opponents on every shift of every game. And when they were sent off to the penalty box night after night, the Broad Street Bullies had the chutzpah to complain that the referees and the league were picking on them because their roughhouse style was so successful. And it actually worked. Remember how popular these guys were. NHL cash registers filled whenever the Flyer goon show came to town. The league had to tone it down a bit, but they wouldn't cancel their highest-rated show. So the refs were obligated to call a looser, more tolerant game. There are referees and fans, both then and now, who really think that a disparity in penalties on the scoresheet means that the game was officiated unfairly. Never mind that Team A is there to play hockey and Team B is bent on mayhem, hacking and tackling and gooning it up all over the ice; if Team B gets 10 or 12 richly deserved penalties and Team A only one or two, *the ref was totally biased, he must have had it in for them.*

Norm MacLean, apparently the only writer at *The Hockey News* in those days with the clear vision and the nerve to state the obvious, hit the nail on the head with his column following that infamous Philadelphia-Toronto playoff riot.

> Flyers have introduced two innovations to the NHL: The designated brawler, and fisticuffs as a part of their overall strategy. A crucial assumption they make is that there's a [limited] number of penalties a referee will call against them. Let's peg it at 20; anything over that would be free of charge.
>
> It's also understood, in the NHL, that an official will shoot for some balance between the penalties imposed on the two sides in any given game. In other words, if Flyers draw 20 minors, then the referee will attempt to find 20 Leafs infractions worthy of penalties. Referee Newell violated both these unwritten rules in the third period and came down with extra severity on the Flyers. Naturally, they're complaining.

The NHL went out and clubbed the noisy, easy-to-see rats of hyper-violence, but the subtler, deadlier fleas of clutch-and-grab lived on, infesting almost every team in hockey. The grey area of borderline penalties—the momentary hold, the glancing hook, the vague interference—that a referee previously might or might not have whistled down became uniformly acceptable. And as the rule book became merely a suggestion book, the NHL began its descent down the slippery slope. If that was okay, how about this little slash across the hands... or this little hug in front of the net... or this catch of an airborne puck and carrying it a couple of strides till I'm out of trouble. As long as the ref is calling the game consistently, it doesn't take players more than a few shifts to get a line on what's acceptable and what isn't. And if the other guys can get away with this or that, you'd be foolish not to sink to that level and use those tactics yourself. For years now, only the most flagrant obstruction fouls have drawn a penalty, and often not even those do.

Somewhere in the NHL front office there's a faint glimmer of awareness. Somebody knows the game on the ice is not what it could be or should be. Somebody realizes that Mario and the game's real fans might have a point. So in every one of the past several years, the NHL has pledged to crack down on obstruction fouls. *We're going to call it tighter,* says the league, *so we're putting the players on alert.* And then, for the first two or three weeks of the season, maybe half the NHL refs call a tight, strict, by-the-book game about half the time, and the other half seem to ignore the new directives altogether, and the players and fans don't know whether the game's really going to go by the book or by the unwritten rules hockey's been played by for 25 years. Then everybody whines about how calling it tight produces dull, slow, choppy hockey with too many whistles and stoppages, the dreaded "parade to the penalty box," and after a few weeks nobody calls it tight at all anymore and everything has quietly slid right back to where it was: dull, slow, choppy hockey with not quite so many whistles and stoppages. And the next season, the dance of half-assed efforts and broken promises starts all over again.

"Early last year," Lemieux said late in his final campaign, "when they were calling the clutching and grabbing, it was fun to be able to skate and make plays. It was more like the hockey I grew up playing. A couple of months later, it went back the other way. That's the biggest factor for retiring now.

"I'll miss the guys. What I won't miss is the way the game is being played."

Mario may be retired, but he isn't alone. Where Bobby Hull had been in the forefront of players outraged at the savagery of hockey in the 1970s, his son Brett now pulls no punches in condemning the clutch-and-grab hockey of the 1990s. Long an outspoken critic of the state of the game, Brett Hull in 1997-98 described the NHL as a "rodeo on ice."

"It's unbelievable," he said. "Why don't they throw out the rule book? And they wonder why the second-greatest player in the history of the game—Mario Lemieux—quit. The league had better wake up. It's disappointing for the game. People better start watching and figure it out. It's embarrassing. How can they let the game be like that? It's a hooking and holding fest."

Hull, a perennial Lady Byng candidate, related the details of an incident in 1997 to illustrate the state of officiating in the NHL. Hull had been high-sticked, opening a cut over his eye, and uncharacteristically retaliated; the instigator went unpunished, but to add insult to injury,

Hull wound up with a minor and a misconduct. "I got 10 for showing [the referee] my eye. I got high-sticked too, and I got the only penalty. Sometimes they miss calls like that, but what about all the stuff that's happened on every shift for the last 10 games? They should try calling the hooking, holding, and mugging that goes on out there."

Hull missed a month's worth of play in 1997-98 after having his wrist broken by a slash from the stick of Tomas Sandstrom. Needless to say, there was no penalty on the play that sidelined one of the great goal scorers of all time. While Hull convalesced, he couldn't see any point in tuning in to NHL games on TV, let alone bothering to take in a game in person. "No, I don't watch much," he declared. "It's too depressing, too boring. The game sucks to watch.

"I wouldn't pay to watch them," he added, warming to the topic. "It's boring. The whole style of the game is terrible. There's so much hooking and holding. There's no flow at all. As soon as a team gets something going, the other team ices it, or dumps it out of the building." Nor did the Golden Brett expect the league to do anything to remedy the situation. "No, I doubt it," he said. "They've got the wrong people in charge."

That kind of unrestrained dissent exasperates and infuriates a lot of people. God bless Brett Hull. Those very comments finally drew the ire of Commissioner Bettman, who got on the horn to the St. Louis front office demanding to know whether team officials would discipline Hull for his remarks. Bettman was told he'd have to do it himself, because the Blues management agreed with Hull.

The NHL made its annual vow to "re-emphasize the importance of calling obstruction" yet again prior to the 1997-98 season, with the customary results—sporadic, half-hearted compliance by some refs, unaltered laxity from others, and within a few weeks, business as usual. A recommitment to the rules crackdown, once NHL play resumed following the Olympics, did offer slight improvement and some hope, but not without receiving impatient criticism.

The main complaint from the hockey media and some of the fans was that the increase in penalty calls resulted in too many stoppages, that it "took the flow out the game." To which we say, *what flow?* We didn't see any; Brett Hull didn't see any; how many games have you yourself seen in the last several years that actually had any real pace and rhythm?

The problem is that the so-called crackdown has, in effect, only been applied in random games, and that's no test of its efficacy at all. Some refs seem willing to call the game according to the rule book. Others don't. A few seem capable of calling it close and calling it fair. Many do not. Hardly any seem either willing or able to call it consistently from one game to another, or even from one period or one shift to the next.

We must digress for a moment. This really has no effect one way or the other on scoring, but the competency of NHL officials has a huge impact on the quality of every game, and the inconsistency of the refereeing in the NHL is a big factor in the public perception of hockey as a major-league sport. Your game isn't going to get respect if your on-ice officials display all the awareness of pro wrestling referees.

Let's be fair. There's probably no sport nearly as tough to officiate as hockey. A baseball umpire stays pretty much rooted to the spot, making calls on slow-developing plays that almost always happen right in front of him. A football official may have to jog around a bit and avoid being stepped on, but each official has to observe only one small section of the field and certain players. A hockey ref, however, skates an endless all-out shift that lasts 60 minutes or more, dodging players and pucks, and trying to catch all the little business going on at 30 miles an hour both in front of and behind him. No referee is ever going to be able to see every little infraction in every game. It's no wonder a lot of them prefer to call it loose and whistle down only the most flagrant and obvious fouls.

Still, you used to be able to expect, at the very least, a consistent performance. Some called it a little tighter, some a little looser, some let just a little more go as it got late in a close game, but the players and the fans knew each referee and knew his style was the same every night. Most refs had a rapport with the players—if both teams gave every indication that they wanted to play a physical game, the ref recognized it and let the little stuff go, and the teams could be counted on not to go too far over the edge. If they showed that they wanted to skate and finesse it, the ref watched it more closely and called any little foul that got in the way of that. And you could talk to those guys—the refs and the players all knew each other; there was a mutual understanding and a mutual respect.

Now you never know what you're going to get. So many refs today run a game like that ex-drill-sergeant substitute teacher you had in Grade 9, who didn't know any of you but regarded you all as disgusting little potential criminals, then let anything go—bullies pounding on bookworms as spitballs and paper planes filled the air—as long as you didn't have the impudence to say anything to the guy. You never know if the refs will call everything or call nothing—and just when you think you do have it figured out, some piddly call comes out of the blue, or something outrageous is overlooked entirely. Why? Has the game gotten so much faster? Aren't we all pretty much agreed that it's actually become *slower* in the last few years? Ask again why that is, though, and you've got half the answer to the officiating question. It's all the clutch-and-grab garbage going on out there that slows the game down—and it goes on so continuously that it really is impossible to call it all. The laxity of the referees' work through the last 25 years, in all these games that could best be described as having been vaguely officiated, has created an almost obligatory anything-goes atmosphere for restraining fouls. If you don't have the puck on the end of your stick, you'd damn well better have your stick wedged in an opponent's armpit.

Nowhere is there such a discrepancy between what's forbidden by the rule book and what's allowed by the game's unwritten rules as in playoff overtime. And if you honestly think about it, the bromide that rationalizes this—*let the players decide it*—is one of the dumbest clichés in hockey. Now nobody—not the players, not the referees, not you, and definitely not us—wants to see a sudden-death playoff confrontation turn on a cheap call, on a penalty for some harmless, incidental infraction that might not even have actually been a foul. Call it a little looser in OT, that's fine. But over the years, this concept expanded to cast a tolerant eye on anything that didn't result in dismemberment. And a lot of good, honest, otherwise knowledgeable fans support this: Let the players decide it! After a certain point, though, this pretty sentiment came to mean let the dirtiest, most graceless practitioners of clutch-and-grab, and not the swift, skilful, artistic players, decide it. Don't the players who can skate and stickhandle and pass and shoot have just as much right to decide the game as those who can only hold and hook and tackle? Why should they, and the game, have to descend to that level? If you're an advocate of the let-the-players-decide-it maxim, where do you draw the line? Or do you draw any line at all? Is no foul too extreme? Should overtime just be a caveman competition?

The other half of the officiating problem is the same one that afflicts the level of playing talent. In the early years of expansion, the NHL carried a staff of 16 or 18 referees, maybe nine or 10 of whom handled nearly every game. Today there are 25 or 30 refs eligible to work NHL games, about 18 or 20 of whom get the bulk of the assignments. Expansion lowers the standard in officiating as well, and there's not a fan reading this who doesn't have his or her own idea as to which referees aren't capable of calling a game at a major-league level. And you can't blame the refs for being a little confused themselves; they call the games according to the guidelines given them by the league—the guidelines that last month told them to let everything but the flagrant and dangerous stuff go, and this month told them to call every damn thing, and last week told them to turn a blind eye to this business and that business but really get tough on offensive interference, and next week will tell them something else again.

Do new rules help? Does technology help? Oh baby. If the road to hell is paved with good intentions, the roadside rest area is shaped like an

NHL goal crease. The anguished uproar over lacklustre play and the lack of scoring in 1997-98 had barely subsided into the dull grumbling of resignation when it erupted again into a deafening outrage over the man-in-the-crease rule and the application of video replay.

These at least were well-meaning changes when they were introduced in 1991. In that year, the goal crease was expanded to European dimensions and players were prohibited from so much as placing their stick in the crease before the puck arrived, changes intended to protect goalkeepers from being run over. When video replay was added, it was meant as a tool to help refs on hard-to-see scoring plays.

We said these ideas were "well-meaning." We didn't say these ideas were "good." The crease didn't need to be enlarged; the rule book already provided ample protection for goaltenders. The problem yet again was simply the failure to enforce the rules. Video replay is another matter. Its arrival smacked of the hyper-cyber-techno world of the NFL, an unpleasant intrusion of futuristic electronics in a place whose rough natural textures had been sublimely epitomized by ice over concrete, the wood of the boards and the sticks, the leather of a skateboot and the cast iron of the goalposts. But the eye in the sky proved to have some value. Did that rocket shot spring back out because it hit the crossbar, or because it hit a tight section of mesh at the back of the net? Did the goalie roll back in time to grab that loose puck before it trickled across the goal line, or didn't he? Now we'd know. In such cases, the camera is useful.

But something happened over the course of seven years. Somehow these two tenuously related notions, linked only by the date of their introduction and the area of the rink they concerned, morphed into one hideous two-headed genetic mutant of a rule. Whose bright idea was it to use the video-replay technology to police not just the goal line but the entire crease and anybody who breathed on it? Can you spell "anal"?

The obsessive-compulsive attention to the spontaneity-killing "man in the crease" rule dampens the sudden joy or pain of every goal with the hanging threat of video review, turning the decisive thrill of any tally into the dreary possibility of laborious judging by committee. The galvanizing jubilation or the crushing disappointment we all once felt with every goal has been blunted, tamed, thinned.

Once upon a time, the back of the net bulged, and we all leapt to our feet, the arena erupting around us as the red light flashed on and the ref pointed in rigid authority. Or the puck trickled across the line as we watched on TV, and we all sprang off the sofa with a roar, hoisting our beer and pizza in triumph and scaring the cat out of the room.

That was then. This is now. "Oh. A goal." Is it? What's the ref say— is he going for the phone? No? So—it's a goal then. Hey. Woo-hoo. That's the reaction now—and that's the best-case scenario. He *is* going to ask for a look at it? Good chance to head for the kitchen or the concession stand. Let us know when we get back whether it was a goal or not. To paraphrase a great American jurist, jubilation delayed is jubilation denied. It doesn't matter if one out of every thirty goals went to review this past year, or one out of six, or one out of a hundred. The possibility of video review drained a measure of excitement out of almost every one of them whether they went to review or not.

The cost of this technological advance in terms of the emotion it takes away from the game would be far too great even if it worked perfectly. Ask fans in Boston or Buffalo or any number of NHL cities how well they think it works. It's not the technology, not the cameras or the video machines—as always, it comes down to the human element. Tim Taylor has absolutely no effect on the play, but his toenail barely overhangs the outline of the crease on P.J. Axelsson's overtime goal—and the play is under review. *No!* The goal is nullified. Peter Bondra stands firmly in the crease jabbing at Dominik Hasek's glove as the puck deflects home—but there will be no review. *The goal stands!* "I don't blame the referee," said Boston's great defenceman Raymond Bourque. "I blame the general managers and the league who have got to get together and do something about that rule, because it's ridiculous."

Ridiculous is right. Speaking of great Boston defencemen, think back to one of the most famous goals ever scored: Bobby Orr's Cup-clinching flight through midair in overtime against St. Louis in 1970. What if the video-review rule had been in effect then? Here's Orr, taking the puck right in front of the Blues' net, Noel Picard bearing down on him... Orr gets the shot away as Picard trips him!... He's flying through the air! Hall lunges!... *He scores!* Orr lands on the ice, he's being mobbed by his teammates! The crowd is going wild! It's Boston's first Stanley Cup in 29 years! Hold it... now the referee is signalling for a look upstairs. We're going to have to wait and see. The question is, "Was Orr's skate in the crease?" Orr gets up and heads over to the bench to await the word. Will it count, or not? Here's one angle, hard to tell. The crowd's quieting down now. Another angle: looks like his skate *might* have been in the crease. Let's run it back and forth a couple of times. The Bruins are standing around awaiting the decision. Here's another angle. There seem to be a couple of inches of ice between Orr's skate and the crease. Mind you, it looks like Orr's stick might have interfered with Hall as he flew past. We'll have to see if the referee is really checking that instead of the crease violation.... And now the signal.... Yes! The goal stands. *Now* the celebration can begin....

Not only does the video-replay aspect of the crease rule throw a wet blanket over the excitement of goal scoring, it's yet another factor in suppressing the amount of goal scoring. Garbage goals and close-in tips represent a significant portion of goals scored—or at least they used to, before players had to tippytoe politely around the perimeter of a crease that encompassed 56 1/2 square feet of ice, almost twice the size of the old 4-by-8-foot rectangle. The Eurocrease was big enough for us to park our cars in—not quite big enough to have reduced Phil Esposito to a 20-goal man, but big enough to have an effect. The NHL trimmed a couple of feet off the sides of the Eurocrease for 1998-99, but the size of the crease was a factor in the preceding few years and the ultrasensitive burglar-alarm system still installed there will continue to be. So add that to your field journal.

But we promised you the biggest reason scoring has dwindled to a sickly trickle—bigger than the crease, bigger than the trap, bigger than the clutch-and-grab, bigger than the drab, endless season, bigger than the diaspora of goal-scoring talent throughout a grossly overexpanded league. What can it be? you plead. What can be that big? Look at the goalies of 1997-98. They were wearing it.

When you look at the gear goalies have been able to strap on during the last few years, you understand the theory. When you look at the statistics, you have the proof. Scoring has plummeted as save percentages have risen, and save percentages have skyrocketed as equipment grew extravagantly large.

The 1990s, well on their way to becoming the Age of the Goaltender, have seen a remarkable change in the numbers goalies have put up league-wide. There are, of course, several reasons for that. One is that goaltenders themselves are better coached now. Where once they were almost an outcast on a team, a strange separate breed left alone to work on their game in isolation, they are today the beneficiary of their own personal adviser and mentor, a goalie coach or "goaltending consultant" who works with his team's netminders to strengthen their mechanics and their psyches and help them develop their own "book" on NHL shooters. It's also likely that, given the league-wide rededication to defence, goalies are benefiting from having to face not only a lower number of shots, but a smaller proportion of shots off difficult odd-man breaks and breakaways. And fear is no longer a factor—faces, necks, and every other vulnerable part of a goalie's body is protected from grotesque injury now, so there's no reason to vomit between periods, develop stomach ulcers, or otherwise freak out in the manner of '50s or '60s goalies.

In addition, today's goaltending equipment is largely made of ultra-lightweight synthetics. The gear may look bulky, but it doesn't feel bulky, at least not in comparison to the sandbags Johnny Bower or Terry Sawchuk had to lug around. All that heavy leather and fabric, soaking up sweat and meltwater, getting hotter and damper and heavier as the game and the season wore on—it fatigues us just thinking about it. *You* try making a split-second kick-save with 50 pounds of soaking-wet equipment lashed onto you.

And it's also possible, although just barely, that there is a glut of goaltending talent. By some random fluke of the gene pool, there just may have been a disproportionate number of very good goalies born between the early 1960s and the late 1970s, destined to dominate today's NHL. We don't buy that, though.

Just look at some Vezina Trophy winners of fairly recent vintage. Tom Barrasso won the Vezina in 1984 while posting a save percentage of .893. John Vanbiesbrouck won it in '86 with an .887 mark. Grant Fuhr took the hardware home in '88 with an .881 figure. Those numbers were all typical for the NHL's best goalies in the 1980s. Now check out some save percentages from 1997-98. Here's Tommy Salo at .906. There's Byron Dafoe at .914. And whoa! Trevor Kidd comes in at .922! And those numbers were typical for almost any goaltender in the last several seasons. Are you going to sit there and let anyone tell you that Kidd, or Dafoe, or Salo, is a better goalie than Barrasso or Beezer or Fuhr were in their best seasons?

Get serious. It's the equipment. The biggest difference between Glenn Hall's job and, say, Trevor Kidd's, is the sheer size of the stuff today's netminders get to hide behind. They look like Transformers, ferchrissake! As they get into the crease for the start of the game, you half expect to hear *Form!: feet! and! legs! Form!: blocker! and! glove!—And I'll form the pads!* The mutation of goaltending equipment into enormous, freakish shapes hasn't been a gradual one. The NHL discreetly amended the rule on equipment before 1989-90, allowing leg pads to balloon by a massive 20 percent, from a 10-inch width to a full foot across. Sure enough, within two years, leaguewide save percentages had risen a full seven points from .881 to .888.

With all due respect to baseball legend Ted Williams, it's goaltending that's the toughest job in all of sports. So you can't blame goalies for looking for any little extra edge, any little legal loophole or omission in the NHL rule book, that might make the task a bit easier. Billy Smith, while with the Islanders, tried wearing what was basically a muu-muu, a size 60 sweater with sleeves that went not from cuff to shoulder and armpit, but from cuff to shoulder and hip. That sweater was later used as a sail on an America's Cup yacht. Tony Esposito used a net-like section of equipment-bag mesh sewn onto his hockey pants, stretching from crotch to knee and from one knee to the other, the year he posted 15 shutouts for Chicago. Not much of a five-hole on that guy.

By 1997-98, every goalie had a size 60 sweater to go with a full set of bloated pads. Buttressed by such massive structural support, journeymen back-up goalies saw their efficiency rise at a dizzying rate: Arturs Irbe, for instance, posted a dismal .860 save percentage in 1995-96, improved to .893 in '96-97, and crested at .907 in '97-98. Over those same three years, Craig Billington went from .867 to .909 to .923!

Philadelphia's Garth Snow was the first to go with those gigantic, looming triangular shoulder pads that proliferated on NHL netminders in 1997-98. What the heck *were* those things, anyway? How could he see off to either side? What did he have on under that sweater, one of those old plywood sandwich boards from the Depression with *Eat at Joe's* painted on it? Either that, or he snuck out of Builder's Home Centre with a 4-by-8 section of wall panelling concealed under his shirt. Go high on him? Hell, he was on his knees, and his shoulders were still higher than the crossbar.

And don't even think about shooting to the glove side. By 1997-98 every goalkeeper had something on the end of his arm that seemed part swimming-pool skim net and part microwave oven. About the same time the leg pads swelled up to a foot in width, equipment manufacturers came up with a new design for the catching glove. The rule book prohibits excess material in the webbing between the thumb and forefinger, but it didn't anticipate the addition of a second pouch and a wide padded board running from the thumb almost to the crook of the elbow. Goalies used to have to snag a shot with a precise thrust of a glove hand clad in something no bigger than an infielder's mitt. After 1989 they could just wave at a shot to the glove side and something the size of a picket sign was sure to block it. Fox Network broadcaster Peter McNab exhibited a then-current version of the gigantic trapper during a televised game in March 1998, contrasting it with the style of glove in vogue 20 years ago. Play-by-play man Jiggs McDonald looked up with a start. "That's half a cow!" he exclaimed.

Behold the numbers. Our chart opposite displays, for each year since the NHL started keeping track of shots and saves in the 1982-83 season, the average number of shots on goal faced by league goaltenders every 60 minutes, and the average save percentage for all goalies in each of those seasons.

NHL shots on goal and save percentage, 1982-83 to 1997-98

	Avg SoG/gp	Avg Sv pct
1982-83	30.6	.875
1983-84	30.3	.873
1984-85	30.1	.874
1985-86	30.7	.874
1986-87	29.6	.880
1987-88	30.1	.880
1988-89	30.1	.879
1989-90	30.0	.881
1990-91	29.4	.886
1991-92	30.1	.888
1992-93	30.7	.885
1993-94	29.9	.895
1994-95	29.0	.901
1995-96	29.9	.898
1996-97	29.4	.905
1997-98	26.9	.906

Avg SoG/gp (Average shots on goal per game played)
includes shots resulting in empty-net goals.
Sv pct does not include empty-net goals or shots on goal
resulting in empty-net goals.

Where did all the scoring go? As the late, great Ted Darling used to say, "It's gotten lost somewhere in the goalie's paraphernalia."

In the summer of 1998 the NHL finally decided to limit the dimensions of that gear, drawing up precise new guidelines regarding the size of sweaters, shoulder pads, pants, and catching gloves. It's a remarkably sensible response on the league's part, and it will be a big help in returning some goals to the game. But you've got to wonder why they stopped there, why they didn't return the old restrictions on the size of the leg pads as well, the enlargement of which sparked this whole trend towards gigantic equipment. Moreover, you've got to wonder what on earth ever prompted them to allow such a major amendment to the regulations on equipment in the first place.

It seems so obvious when you just sit down and take some time to think about it. We can all see that the NHL's on-ice product is a thin shadow of what it once was. Why? Because the season drags on forever, filled with meaningless, poorly officiated games against ridiculous teams full of minor-league players—games interrupted and dictated by the meddlesome presence of TV technology. And in those games, there is no action, let alone any scoring. And why is that? Because the desperate lack of scoring talent in an expansion-weakened league leaves teams little choice but to play defence to the exclusion of offence; because a league-mandated inattention to the rule book allows play to degenerate nightly into a dull slow-dance of clutch-and-grab; and because goalies now have an overpowering upper hand, thanks to an ironic overattention to one small section of the rule book and the radical enlargement of goaltending equipment.

Hull related the conversation he had with Bettman following Hull's January remarks on the deteriorated condition of NHL play. "Bettman got on the phone, and he said, 'We see everything you do; we're addressing it. But we don't need you to say the game sucks.'

"And he's right," Hull said. "But I was just thinking about the fans."

At least somebody was.

Chapter 4

the malling
of the nhl

"There's only going to be one Forum. This place is like a
church for a lot of fans across Canada."

—Guy Lafleur

Once, going to an NHL game was a magical experience, full of anticipation and ritual. The old arenas were august temples, most of them distinctive, stylish edifices of stone and brick; you entered beneath a great
artistic facade, through massive doors that at one side of the building
might be of riveted iron, the doors to the vaults of the mountain kings,
and a block away on the other side of the building might be detailed
with art deco glass and burnished brass furniture. Once inside and out
of the snow, you felt privileged to become part of a tradition, to be surrounded by monolithic walls that had been witness through so many

years to the exploits of the game's greats, to the lifting of the Stanley Cup, and to the passion of countless fans, the team's colours coursing through their veins. Inside, the stone floors and stairways, worn smooth over decades by the shoes of 10 million faithful, wound at odd angles around unexpected turns and down narrow passageways as deliciously mysterious as the secret chambers of the pyramids. When a dim, grey-walled tunnel at last opened suddenly onto the rink, the sight was exhilarating: the brilliant white glare of an immense sheet of ice, a pristine frozen lake enclosed by vast cliffs of seats teeming with fans abuzz with expectation—the fresh discovery, even seen for the thousandth time, of a spectacular hidden world.

There was a palpable electricity in the air; fans knew the game and knew one another, talking hockey in shadowy alcoves of crowded corridors over a hot dog and a beer and a cigar. Inside the rink, fans sat chock-a-block in wooden seats whose soft patina felt like history, seats clustered so close to the ice that even in the balcony you were close enough to read the expressions on the players' faces. You knew all the players on every team, and every game meant something, and every goal was a goal, by god, and dammit, every penalty was a penalty, and every game left a memory.

Now, the game's at a gigantic modern sportsplex as anonymous and undistinguished as every other gigantic modern sportsplex, a bland new megamall with broad tiled concourses, widening into food courts that offer yogurt and wine coolers, and vast Gap-like boutiques selling racks of overpriced team jerseys and jackets boasting whatever new logo and colours the team is wearing this month. Once inside, glad only to have escaped the sweltering subtropical heat, we find great expanses of thinly populated interior space, with all the bustle and vitality of a major airline terminal at four in the morning. A few yuppies in Armani suits and trench coats wander the quiet concourse like mall zombies, talking not about the game but about mutual funds and departmental restructuring. They'll get to their seats 10 minutes after the game starts and leave 10 minutes before it's over. They've never heard of Jean Beliveau or Tim Horton; they could care less who's playing or who wins tonight. Hey, they're probably NHL executives.

All conversation stops as we enter the stands because we're drowned out by the ceaseless, ear-splitting din of piped-in dancetronic rock music. Your hard plastic seat is somewhere in a bowl the size of a football stadium, gently angled as low and level as a movie theatre, so you'd better have brought your binoculars. Oh, never mind, you can watch the whole game on TV, on the giant Megatron screens, and ignore the actual ice completely. Some ridiculous giant Muppet gambols moronically through sections of empty seats in a pathetic effort to enliven the scattered crowd. And somewhere out there on that white postage stamp of ice, a little below and a mile away, your team of ants is playing some other team of ants from New Mexico or Louisiana, and if once or twice all night someone gets through all the clutching and grabbing and hooking and holding that passes for defence and actually puts the puck in the net, we'll all wait five minutes for the video review committee to decide if it was actually a goal. And if we're lucky, we might be able to afford to do this one time next year, too, assuming the team's still here and hasn't relocated to Houston or Jacksonville or

Memphis—and assuming we're still interested. *This isn't what we came to see.*

All the great old buildings are gone now, every one of them abandoned or razed but for Maple Leaf Gardens; by the time you read this, the Gardens may be deserted too. It's too late to save them, too late to do anything but elegize them. In just the first five years of Gary Bettman's commissionership, Chicago Stadium, Boston Garden, the Montreal Forum, the St. Louis Arena, and Buffalo's Memorial Auditorium have all been sacked. The timing of their fall, in such rapid order upon Bettman's arrival, was reminiscent of the vandalism and desecration of a fallen city's temples by a conquering foreign army.

Of course, the plans to dispose of each hallowed edifice had already been in the works well before Bettman's arrival. The real justification was that none of them could be retrofitted to accommodate banks of luxury suites, which bring in millions in corporate dollars each year for the franchise playing in that building, income the teams claim is necessary to allow them to stay competitive. Maybe that's true. But it would have been a little easier for all of us as fans to accept if the owners and the league had expressed the slightest sense of regret, any jot of sympathy, if they had at least been up front about the money being their sole motivation.

Instead, what we read and heard were mostly their efforts to rationalize for us the desertion of the marvellous, atmospheric old arenas of stone, wood, and fabric. The ancient buildings, elegant and dignified, that held so many memories of great games, great players, great plays, of great times for all of us fans with friends and family, were endlessly denigrated as "dirty," "cramped," "stuffy," "inadequate," "antiquated," "forbidding," and so on, while the gigantic new arenas of aluminum and plastic that replaced them, with their horrid sight lines, warehouse ambience, and millionaires-only, thank you, ticket prices, were relentlessly hyped as positive "fan-friendly" developments.

Disgracefully, most of the hockey media swallowed this propaganda whole and regurgitated it daily, based not on how truly great, or supposedly awful, these old places were for any of us as fans to enjoy a game, but on how much they disliked the press-box accommodations. The Boston Garden press box was overcrowded and you could snag yourself on the plywood shelf that served as the work table, the press box at the Aud was hard to get to and didn't have enough TV monitors, yadda yadda yadda.... Well boo-hoo-hoo. The Garden press box *was* overcrowded, and it was one of the best views we've ever had of a game. The wrought-iron gondola at the Aud was great too.

Worse than the media, though, were those fans who also turned into mindless sheep and bought everything the owners and the media told them; the building they'd loved for years was suddenly, somehow, yes! dirty and stuffy and inadequate. Money must be found for a new temple! Where the proposal of an extra few pennies a year in taxes to fund schools or libraries or a clean environment had been cause for armed insurrection, the idea of coughing up millions of tax dollars to fund construction of a new playpen for a billionaire owner became a happy civic duty.

Upon securing their new stadium deals, ownership in Chicago and Montreal did an abrupt about-face and pushed the nostalgia button, promoting the hell out of their old arenas as the setting for noble scenes of joy and glory. This late-found appreciation for the old buildings almost made the owners seem human, until you realized it was all meant only to ensure sell-out crowds over the arenas' final year and flog all sorts of newly minted nostalgia-themed merchandise.

Ask the fans in Chicago or Buffalo whether their new rink is a better place to watch hockey than what they had. Some of them are still in denial; they'll try to tell you that the new building actually is an improvement—there are more concession stands, and those titanic TV monitors, y'know, and, um… because to admit otherwise is to admit how naive they were in believing that the new building would have one single positive effect beyond keeping their team from bolting town for some other community dumb enough to think the millions in taxes necessary to build a new arena are a good financial investment.

We knew, the moment the decision was made to move forward—or backward, really—with plans to replace each of the old rinks, that the proposed new sportsplex wouldn't hold a candle to what had come before. Architects and city planners and team management actually had the brass to smile and outright lie to the public about how the new building would be better for the fans, to make the mutually exclusive promises that it would both be roomier and have better sight lines. The evolution of public safety laws in the 50 or 60 years or more since the old arenas were built mandated that the new rinks be roomier and that the sight lines be worse—as they must inevitably be anyway, once the seats have to be made larger and spread farther apart, and architects are no longer allowed to design and build auditoriums in which the stands are pitched upward at a 45-degree angle. Mostly, however, the very rea-son these new rinks were being built in the first place obviated any hope of a better view for ordinary fans. Luxury boxes and corporate suites would be the overriding priority; those places—inaccessible to normal working-class humans—would occupy all the very best spots and afford all the very best views. Everyone seated above them in the balcony level would just have to deal with squinting at the little squiggles on the ice from 30 or 40 feet higher than in the old buildings.

Okay, maybe we've romanticized the old arenas just a tad. There weren't really nymphs and centaurs inside, frolicking under a celestial light. Well, there were a few in the Aud, but that was the only one. The point is, any fan who's being honest knows that the new arenas are dreadful in comparison to the old buildings, where every seat in the building felt close to the action, where there was always excitement in the air. And we knew the quirks and stories of the other teams' arenas, too, even if we'd never been there, just from listening to the colour commentary on radio or watching games broadcast from those build-ings. We loved them not just for their history and the memories that were created in them, but because each was unique, each had a person-ality. You could be dropped into any one of them and know instantly where you were without ever having to see a team crest—the Forum, richly red, with the amenities of a fine West End theatre in the lobby; the Boston Garden, with its mustard yellow corridors and balcony seats cantilevered at crazy angles in the corners; Chicago Stadium, red and charcoal grey, with its narrow mezzanine and brilliant golden organ loft; the Aud, with its maze of grey and blue corridors, its yellow walls and railings, and the daunting steepness of its huge orange balcony—and before them, Detroit's Olympia and the welcoming warmth of its lobby, and even the Spectrum in Philadelphia, the blood-red Berchtesgaden of the NHL, that too had a distinctive look and feel and yes, it too was a great place to watch a game. When you went to those buildings and actually saw a game there in person, it was a special experience, like visiting the Parliament buildings or the Old North Church or anyplace where some important episode in history had physically played out.

Who can feel that way about any of the many megastadiums that keep springing up like the fast-forward construction montage outside Rod Taylor's parlour window in *The Time Machine?* What distinguishes any one of the new "sports complexes" from any other? Nothing. The United Center, the Fleet Center, the MCI Center, the Molson Centre, the Corel Centre, the CoreStates Center, the Kiel Center, the Air Canada Centre, the National Car Rental Center for cryin' out loud— why the hell so many "centres," anyway? Probably because they're all but interchangeable, just one big pastel suburban shopping mall after another, where you're so far from the ice that the sound of an errant slapshot caroming off the end boards doesn't reach your ears until two seconds after you see it.

Fans in Toronto—any fans anywhere, really—who want to experience for the last time what it's like to enjoy an NHL game in an arena with a life and a personality of its own had better be sure to make their way to a Leaf game before the 1998-99 season is through. Take some time to make your way around the wonderful old blue lady on Carlton Street. Savour those great player portraits, part George Hurrell celebrity glamour photo, part Eastern Orthodox church icon. Check out the blue-suited ushers, some of whom seem to have worked there since the Leafs were the St. Patricks (but mind which ones you drop your ticket stub in front of). Enjoy the terrific sight lines, from centre ice or behind the goal, from high up or down low. Enjoy the view from the sharply angled corners and from the tight space of standing room. There won't be any of that in your new rink, or in any rink ever again.

What there will be in your new rink is lots of noise. Not so much from the fans, where it should be coming from—because there's not that much to cheer about—but from the public address speakers. At every game, at every arena, during every possible nanosecond of every stoppage of play, we are all subjected to the relentless ear-shattering blast of garbled snippets of rock and pop music through tinny, echoing PA systems, making conversation and analysis and even heckling too difficult to even bother attempting. It's so bad, so annoying, and so actually painful, that it was the deciding factor for one of us when he gave up his season tickets a couple of years ago. They were too expensive, but still… the team sucked, and yet…. He was leaning towards renewing anyway, because he enjoyed the banter and the jokes and discussing the team and the game with the friends with whom he'd shared the block of seats for many years. But the team took even that away. Conversation was no longer possible under the canned music's ceaseless assault.

Frankly, we weren't even that keen on most of the organ music that used to occasionally punctuate an NHL game. A few organists around the league had a sense of restraint and played only when the crowd had been lulled into a torpor by a stretch of uneventful hockey; a few had a sense of humour and could actually make an amusing musical comment on something happening on the ice. Others just noodled pointlessly; mostly it was just filler, yet even at that it contributed a certain friendly intimacy to the ambience of the game, and was a nocturne by Chopin compared to the piercing screech of '80s metal that now fills the acoustically unfriendly space of a hockey arena.

Who decided that abruptly truncated excerpts from the Top 40, blasting out louder than a jackhammer, was a good thing? One of us can't even take his father to a game anymore, because Dad won't put up with that crap. Granted, Dad likes Perry Como and the Mills Brothers, but we grew up on Zeppelin and The Who and still listen to all sorts of loud bizarre rock, and we can't stand the noise at the arenas either. It's not music—not when it's played in fragmented sound bites completely unrelated to what's happening on the ice, not when it's rendered into jagged indecipherable noise by being cranked at 120 decibels, not when it causes actual physical discomfort, not when it's an unwanted intrusion that utterly drowns out all hope of conversation, not when you can't be heard over it despite shouting as loud as you can to someone sitting right next to you. That's not music, that's not entertainment; it's more like some sort of torture employed to brainwash political prisoners. And in that capacity, it's working, if the intent is to make us less likely to attend an NHL game.

Dare we wonder aloud why the league hasn't just gone ahead and permitted clubs to pump out this eardrum-shredding din throughout the entire game, as is the practice in box lacrosse and indoor soccer? Could any fan enjoy this? Do we actually need any of it? Have we become so mindless that we actually require deafening canned music to inspire us to cheer, or, less painful but more insulting, those idiotic electronic animations on the scoreboard exhorting us to "Get Loud!" or "Make Some Noise!" or "Clap!"?

If we are indeed confused about anything, it might only be the identity of the teams playing. Who *are* those guys? Check your ticket stub or the TV listings, because you sure can't tell at a glance, or even with a long stare. A uniform used to mean something, it used to stand for something; your allegiance to the team's colours was like your allegiance to the flag. Now teams change uniforms more often than most people change their underwear in an unabashed grab for marketing dollars, replacing crests and colours fans have cheered for a generation with garish cacophonies of colour and cartoonish logos slapped together out of a computer clip-art file.

The *bleu, blanc, et rouge*—that *means* Montreal, that *is* the Canadiens. The stately blue and white of the Maple Leafs, the bold, uncomplicated red and white of Detroit, the menacing black and yellow of the Bruins—whether you love them or hate them, whether they're currently a Cup contender or rebuilding in the basement, each of these is a team with a history, with an identity; they're unimaginable in any other colours. Can you picture the Habs in green and black, or the Leafs in red, silver, and teal? How about adding some big diagonal black and turquoise stripes to the Red Wings sweater? Better yet, change the crests... get rid of that boring "CH" thing. Make it a cartoon figure, a goofy caricature of a Québecois in a tuque, brandishing a hockey stick...

and that stupid leaf, the kids won't buy that—make it a *fierce* leaf, with huge nasty teeth, *biting* a hockey stick.

Crayola's big 64-crayon box doesn't have some of the colours teams are wearing today. Just what are the Phoenix Coyotes' colours? Burnt umber, raw umber, forest green, periwinkle, and flesh? It's not like all the good colours were already taken or anything: half the teams in the NHL wear black on the road. Black used to be the Bruins, and that was that. Then Pittsburgh ditched their industrial-league powder-blue sweaters and went to black. Okay, we'll give them that one; they are the Penguins, after all. But was black the only idea Los Angeles could cook up when they decided to open a new chapter with the Gretzky era? Were the NFL Raiders the best the Kings could find for a fashion role model? Was black the only colour Ottawa could think of when they rejoined the NHL? Was black really the best that Buffalo could come up with when they betrayed 26 years of blue and gold? Tampa, Phoenix, Dallas, Vancouver, and now Chicago, Washington, Philadelphia, and even Calgary—black. How startlingly, daringly original. Aren't a team's colours supposed to *distinguish* it from other teams? Well, give them another season; the minute someone in some team's marketing department realizes their replica sweaters didn't outsell some other team's replica sweaters, they'll change the colours again. Unfortunately, it'll probably be the marketing department in New Jersey, or Edmonton, and they'll change to *black*.

Wacky colours and dreary, repetitive overuse of black aside, the problem with the designs is the nauseating train wreck of stripes and waves and diagonals and triangles and dashes that festoons almost every uniform. Note to designers: when there are more bars and stripes and patches and bands and inserts than there is solid base colour, *you're trying way too hard*. Pick whatever colours you want, but when you're done, try to have something that looks like a uniform, not like the knee-deep pile of torn giftwrap littering your living room at the end of Christmas morning.

If we ever get our hands on the first fashion design genius who took the traditional horizontal stripe around a sweater's waist and set it on a naughty, debonair angle, or bent it into a sprightly, vivacious wave, or broke it into sassy, zesty dashes, they'll be looking for their T-square and airbrush with the help of a proctologist. Who decided shoulder yokes are pointy? Since when do pinstripes belong on a hockey sweater? How many stripes does St. Louis need—and what was that giant red cummerbund draped from armpit to hip? Something Burt Lancaster wouldn't wear in *The Crimson Pirate*? Why did Buffalo and half a dozen other teams decide to wear box lacrosse jerseys instead of hockey sweaters? So many questions—and we haven't even started on the crests.

We were running a playoff pool where we worked back in 1987, and a friend wanted in. He's from Macedonia, a huge soccer fan, but had only recently become a big fan of hockey, having emigrated to the States just a few years earlier. Without hesitation, he picked Philadelphia—a solid but far from prohibitive choice—to make it through to the Final. Why so sure? we asked. "*This*, man," he laughed, pinching the front of his shirt and flapping it at us. "The crest."

He understood the power that tradition and bold simplicity give a symbolic image, the way a crest helps inspire the team wearing it and helps intimidate their opponents. The crests of every one of the Original Six teams have that power. Most of the first wave of expansion teams had it. And since then, we've been forced to witness a cavalcade of violence-themed kiddie cartoons and the just plain incomprehensible, inspiring, at best, complete indifference, and, at worst, embarrassment for the players obligated to wear them. Consider the iconic uniforms and crests of yesteryear—the strong, graceful arc of the Montreal "C," the industrial might of the Boston "B," the stern profile of the Indian chief Black Hawk, the Red Wings' quasi-Victorian hieroglyph—these things say hockey, firmly, plainly, and unmistakably; these things *are* hockey. The Rangers spell their name out in capital block letters, emboldened by a 3-D drop-shadow or emblazoned on a shield; Toronto retains its heritage even in the geometrically simplified version of the Maple Leaf. Not a single lunging beast or little hockey stick among them. Yet if these debuted today, *The Hockey News*'s annual "pro logo ranking" would probably rate them 22nd through 27th in the NHL—"they don't project an image of toughness," or "you can't tell they belong to a hockey team" because they don't feature a snarling carnivore chomping its way through a hockey stick.

Lame and ugly design and hyperaggressive heraldry aren't the exclusive province of the NHL's most recent additions; they've merely made it *de rigueur*. Was it some sort of inside joke in Washington when the team entered the league in 1974 with "capitals" spelled out across the players' chests in *lower-case letters*? And with the "t" forming a little hockey stick, of course. Washington finally ditched those duds a couple of years ago for uniforms featuring a stylized, diving eagle, a crest nearly identical to that of the U.S. Express Mail service—perhaps hoping to suggest to opponents that Washington players might go postal on them. Norm Green tipped his hand that he had no intention of keeping the North Stars in Minnesota when he wrested the title for lamest logo away from the Caps. Well before the team was dragged to Dallas, Minnesota had already given up the clean, '60s, World's Fair graphics of the North Star "N" and shortened their name to the incomparably generic "Stars." We could go on, but we'll just say this: It's because of artistic standards this low that you eventually wind up with the utterly inscrutable blur—is it an ink-blot test? is it a toilet swirl?—that stains the sweaters of the Carolina Hurricanes. And you can't expect those standards to improve, when you recall that one of the three precon- ceived ideas Bettman had when he took office was to discard the NHL's own time-honoured heraldic shield and replace it with some zippy red- white-and-blue imitation of the NBA and Major League Baseball logos.

Canadian teams, though, aren't without artistic sin either. What's up with Ottawa? Fuzzy thinking in national capitals must extend well beyond politics. They're the Senators. The *Senators*. Why is the guy on their crest a *centurion*? Vancouver, as best as we can decipher, because you have to get your face right up to it to figure it out, is an angry killer whale with giant teeth, leaping out of the icy water, only to be awk- wardly contorted into a crude "C." They couldn't have been thinking of San Jose's logo when they created that, could they? You know—San Jose, the Sharks, whose jerseys and jackets and caps and keychains and assorted merchandise were the NHL's hottest-selling property for their first several years in the league, who made an estimated US$200 million in ancillary sales of gear and accessories in the first two years of their existence? San Jose, whose repugnantly stupid logo is the one that really ignited this whole trend towards embroidered and silk-screened cartoon mayhem? San Jose. It's a shark. Fine. So show a shark already. But why is he biting a stick in half? If that's his own stick, he's going to be at quite a disadvantage.

The evolutionary line of descent that originates with the Sharks immediately divides into two branches: the stupid, ferocious cartoon animal, which is designed to appeal to 12-year-olds, and the stupid, cute cartoon animal, which is designed to appeal to 6-year-olds. The Florida Panthers were the first to take the former tack; the outstretched talons of the Washington eagle mark it as a relative, Buffalo's demonic goat falls into this category, and the astoundingly hackneyed logo of the Nashville Predators is the newest member of the family. The snarling cat head of the Predators logo (Or *is* it snarling? Actually, it seems to be gagging; perhaps it's getting ready to hack up a hairball.) could be switched with that of either of the NFL's own recent expansion franchises, the Jacksonville Jaguars and the Carolina Cougars, and no one would even notice. It is, in fact, an unabashed copycat, so to speak, of the logo of the San Jose SaberCats of the Arena Football League, and the name itself, just as tellingly, is the same as that of another arena football team, the Orlando Predators. Minutes after being selected by Nashville in the June 1998 expansion draft, former Devils goalie Mike Dunham was asked if he could say just what the figure representing the Predators was. "I do not know," Dunham said with a grin. Having pulled on a Nashville jersey, Dunham examined the crest and ventured, "It's an animal with a big tooth." But, he cautioned, "If I had to explain it to school kids, I couldn't do it."

Of course, the minor leagues continue to spread these mutations, as AHL, IHL, and ECHL teams include rampaging hunter-killers like those pouncing from the chests of the Worcester IceCats, Tallahassee TigerSharks, Detroit Vipers, Chicago Wolves, Hartford Wolfpack, Pee Dee Pride, and that totem of pubescent *Spawn* readers, the Beast of New Haven, among others.

Disney, that corporate object of NHL desire, was given carte blanche to wipe its big yellow birdfeet on NHL tradition when it decided an NHL franchise might be an amusing toy for promoting its *Mighty Ducks* movies. With complete disregard for tradition or dignity, the Mighty Ducks of Anaheim arrived, with a name all at once inappropriate, pompous, and preposterous, and with an angrily determined—but gently unthreatening—Donald Duck goalie-mask logo. This opened the door for the Columbus Blue Jackets and their faddish imitation of the NBA Charlotte Hornets' own adorably pugnacious insect logo, and begat cute, cuddly minor-league offspring like the happy, roly-poly critters adorning the jerseys of Orlando SolarBears, San Antonio Dragons, Cleveland LumberJacks, Charlotte Checkers, and so on.

The whole look of hockey has become unrelievedly tacky and bush league. Why does almost every team need so many patches and appliqués and secondary crests and logos slapped all over their sweaters that the players look like NASCAR drivers? Soon we can expect NHL players, like players in European leagues, will indeed be circling around in sweaters that carry actual advertising on them, finally camouflaging them entirely amid dasher boards and ice already littered with advertising. This was an intriguing novelty to us when we watched international hockey as kids; European ads painted on the boards, reading *ei, ei, ei, Verpoorten* and *ja, ja, Jagermeister* enhanced the cosmopolitan atmosphere of the tournaments. But like borscht or lutefisk, it was merely something to be sampled on those rare occasions in the spirit of the intercultural festival; a steady diet of it would make you blow chunks. Yet sure enough, what do we have in the NHL now? That's right, the boards, wallpapered 200 feet up one side and 200 feet down the other and 85 feet across from corner to corner behind both goals, with ad after ad after ad, the ice itself painted with ads for moving companies and ads for printing companies and ads for banks, ads on the clocks, ads on the Megatron, the walls behind the team benches sprayed with cola ads, the space inside the penalty boxes spattered with bubble-gum ads, an ad for one or another brand of beer glued onto the back of every damn seat in the whole damn arena staring up at us through the whole damn game. And the message of every ad is the same: *it's not about the hockey, stupid, it's only about the money.* "We've talked to an advertiser about buying the space on the goalposts and the crossbar," Toronto Maple Leafs marketing director Bill Cluff told *The Hockey News* in 1992. "We've also looked at the possibility of stamping a logo into the mesh of the net. The NHL doesn't permit that now, but it's a possibility." Don't think they've given up on the idea.

So far we haven't gotten around to insulting the Tampa Bay Lightning, whose most heinous crime is neither their clumsily drawn logo nor the illegible, suburban mailbox lettering on their sweaters. No,

Tampa are guilty of spreading to the NHL the dread contagion of the singular collective noun, a disease they contracted, predictably enough, from the NBA, where entities like the Miami Heat and Orlando Magic also ponce about the peninsula. Patient Zero for this pathogen, now endemic throughout professional sports, appears to have been the Dallas Tornado of the United Soccer Association—forerunner of the North American Soccer League—as far back as 1967. The San Antonio Thunder and Houston Hurricane of the NASL soon followed. Leave it to teams from Texas to come up with something this stupid. Soon soccer and indoor soccer and fly-by-night wannabe leagues in all sorts of sports, like the NFL's doomed rivals, the World Football League and the United States Football League, were crawling with things like the Surf and the Gold and the Blitz and the Fury and the Express—not to forget or forgive the Toronto Blizzard and the Montreal Manic.

Over the years there's been Fever and Sting, Force and Blast, Inferno and Fog, and even the Philadelphia Bell; today the World League of American Football, arena football, Major League Soccer, the Women's National Basketball Association and American Basketball League, indoor soccer and roller hockey are riddled with stuff like the Ambush, the Attack, the Rage, the Rampage, the Shock, the Impact, the Crunch, the Wave, the Clash, the Burn, the Fire, the Mutiny, the Spirit, the Liberty, the Fusion, the Galaxy—every one of them the purulent symptom of teams and leagues that know they're second-rate and are pathetically desperate for any sort of attention, every instance among them indelibly marking their sport as a marginal minor-league amusement.

Hockey, thankfully, had long remained above all this, immune to the epidemic, certainly at the NHL level—until the arrival of the Lightning. With Tampa contaminating the NHL—and minor pro hockey already infected with nomenclature including the Las Vegas Thunder, Columbus Chill, Indianapolis Ice, Toledo Storm, Syracuse Crunch, and New Orleans Brass—Colorado, not so much inspired as given licence, were free to rename the pirated Quebec Nordiques as the Avalanche. The NHL's immune system had been fatally compromised; soon it'll be suffering from the most embarrassing affliction yet, the Minnesota Wild.

The Minnesota Wild *what*? Wildmen? Wildcats? Wild cards? What candidates did this contest winner beat? "The Minnesota Adverb"? Presumably, the mascot for "the Wild" will be known as The Fierce. Look, you're Canadiens or Americans, or Bulldogs or Bruins, or Rangers or Islanders, or Lions or Tigers or Bears, okay? You're not a Lightning, or a Heat, or a Wild, or any other temperature inversion or weather pattern or non-specific verb or adjective.

Team names are just one small component of a far more wide-ranging degeneration of the entire language of the game. The vernacular of hockey, one more wonderful thing that makes the game unique, has been profoundly corrupted by terminology lifted from other American sports and inaptly, incessantly applied to hockey by witless American sportscasters and sportswriters. Hockey is being basketballized, by linguistic garbage like "power forward," "shot clock," "post-up," "put-back," and "backdoor play," and footballized, by "quarterback" and "long bomb"; generic American phraseology like "jersey," "logo," "locker room," "box score," and the hopelessly mixed metaphor of the "home run pass" now pervade discussion of the game even in Canada. Must we, like Catalonians during the Franco regime, be forbidden even to speak our own language under the oppressive heel of the giant basketball sneaker that pins our necks to the ground? Make this your mantra: hockey players wear *sweaters*, adorned with *crests*, and dress in a dressing room where there are *no lockers to be found*. They make smart, heady passes, sometimes even long head-man passes, and take shots that are tallied on a shot counter, *which has no timing device of any kind*. Need we continue?

Bettman's 1993 decision to rename—with bland compass-point titles that refer solely to U.S. geography—the Prince of Wales and Clarence Campbell Conferences and the Adams, Patrick, Norris, and Smythe Divisions, was another baseless, wrong-headed move which served only to further destroy any evidence of hockey's history. The men who had been honoured with those titles may often have been undeserving choices, but at least the game's legacy was being kept out front, and each name became synonymous with a certain style of play. Too confusing for the fans, though, said the NHL.

Always, always, this relentless dumbing down of the game, this push to make it "accessible" to the great unwashed of the American audience. God bless Brian McFarlane, who's done as much as anyone to tell the story of hockey and keep the game's history alive; we can't really blame him for his creation of Peter Puck in the early years of expansion. As irritating as that gormless little vulcanized rubber imp was, condescendingly instructing us in the unfathomable subtleties of icing and offsides, God only knows what NBC and Hanna-Barbera, without McFarlane's input, would have cooked up on their own to "explain" hockey to the U.S. television audience of the early '70s.

What's to explain? This isn't 43-Man Squamish, the hilariously convoluted game invented by *Mad Magazine* back in the 1960s as a satire of international sports. It's hockey. How hard is it to follow? How hard is it to grasp? Sure, it may take a little time to learn to appreciate the finer points of backchecking or to realize how the lone defender back should play a two-on-one, but how many baseball fans can explain the balk rule or the infield fly rule with concision and certainty? How many football fans can precisely diagram the outside linebacker's coverage responsibilities on a safety blitz? Naturally a deeper understanding of rules and strategies enhances your ability to follow and interact with a game, but how much do you really need to know to enjoy hockey, to enjoy any game, at a basic level?

We didn't need to be Dick Irvin and Sam Pollock to be attracted to the game; we were drawn to it the minute we first saw it, by the speed, and the skill, and the very fact that it was so different from anything else we'd seen. You don't become a fan of a sport because it sort of looks a lot like another sport; you don't love hockey because it looks or sounds or feels like basketball, or football, or indoor soccer, or 43-Man Squamish. You love it precisely because it's *different* from those things, because it has its own special sights and sounds, its own style and strategies, its own history and language.

But every single thing done to promote and market hockey has taken just the opposite approach. Just think of the way the NHL has treated its own history. Those nostalgic little kinescope sound bites "From the Archives" on "Hockey Night in Canada," with Ward Cornell interviewing Dick Duff or Pierre Pilote, may be merely amusing to Canadian fans—but to us, tuning in from just across the border, they're as rare and fascinating as discovering a sound-on-film interview with One-Eyed Frank McGee or Jules Verne or Sir Wilfrid Laurier. That's because you never, ever, ever get any sense of anything of the game's heritage on any American hockey telecast, local or national, anywhere. Ever.

Baseball can't get *enough* of grainy, slow-motion, distressed-film images of Lou Gehrig and Joe DiMaggio, the sense-of-awe soundtrack from *The Natural* playing underneath them, on its televised games: Baseball!, and that's literally about all it says in so many worshipfully intoned words. But it speaks volumes, all in equally hushed reverence: baseball, it's America, it's Dad and Granddad, it's the flag waving in the breeze, it's history, it's peanuts and Cracker Jacks, it's your legacy and your birthright. It's the stuff of 27-hour-long Ken Burns documentaries and dozens of new coffee-table books every year on the St. Louis Browns or the 1941 pennant race or Mickey Mantle or baseball in the 19th century or the life of Branch Rickey.

Football, served so superbly by its brilliant and prolific NFL Films operation, loves to trot out digitally restored 8-millimetre black-and-white film of Bobby Layne and Chuck Bednarik and Paul Warfield, scored with dramatic, rousing orchestrations and narrated with the god-like stentorian tones of John Facenda and his imitators, every bit as much and every bit as often as it likes to run those montages of this season's spine-snapping, spleen-jellying collisions.

Basketball, currently the biggest, craziest noise on the North American sporting scene, never got more interest and positive publicity for itself than in 1997, when the NBA trumpeted the selection of its 50 Greatest Players of All Time to spotlight the league's 50th anniversary. The NBA did such a great job of positioning this overview of its history in the media, even people who hate basketball almost as much as we do looked forward to seeing the final roster; they couldn't avoid hearing about the list when it was unveiled, and they read it and debated its merits for weeks. And now the NBA is on a retro kick, celebrating its lean and goofy years of the '70s with renewed appreciation for Dr. J, giant Afros, and hot pants. The NBA has come late to embracing its history, but it's doing it extremely well.

But if you watch hockey on American TV, you'd never know the NHL existed before Gretzky started playing, you might not even get a sense that the game itself existed before the Mighty Ducks took to the ice. Hockey's history, so well enshrined and sustained in the excellent Hall of Fame in Toronto, is of no interest to American networks or apparently to the NHL itself. The league's attitude doesn't seem to have changed one whit since 20 years ago, when it was summed up for us with hideous perfection by an editor for *Goal* magazine, then the NHL's official game program. We'd proposed to write and illustrate a series of pieces that would tell the stories of great Hall of Famers who played from the 19th century through the Original Six era. The editor all but snorted in sincere contempt at the idea. "Nobody," he informed us, "gives a shit about Cyclone Taylor."

So, instead, network broadcasts and NHL commercials focus on—

acck!—"power forwards": giant roughneck players like Lindros and Shanahan and Tkachuk smash into each other in blinding MTV-style montages of collision after collision, plainly meant to evoke NFL ads, featuring gigantic steroid-gorged linemen who smash into each other in blinding MTV-style montages of collision after collision. See? Watch hockey! It's just like football! Other spots highlight the few skilled speedsters in the game, like Jagr and Selanne, their breakaway chance fragmented into a hiccupping series of fraction-of-a-second stop-action stills, copying the NBA ads featuring Michael Jordan or whomever launching himself from the foul line towards a dunk shot in a rapid set of freeze-frame images. Look! Watch hockey! It's just like basketball! All the while, the promotional hype for an upcoming game, backed by the sound of apocalyptic rock chords, is read by some narrator who inevitably sounds like the guy that tells us nitro-burning funny cars will be drag-racing at the Speedway on Sunday!! Sunday!! Sunday!! See all the ads! Listen to all that noise! Feel all the testosterone!

Of more concern is the NHL's failure of imagination even when it does try to break out of cliché mode for a promotional campaign. The NHL comes up with a bright idea, and then, as if powerless to resist some neurotic fixation, veers off in precisely the wrong direction. For the 1998 Stanley Cup playoffs, someone at Fox thought, "Let's get a respected film director to shoot some entertaining hockey promos featuring a well-known comedian." Atom Egoyan and Rick Moranis? Guy Maddin and Eddie Shack? Heck no. Let's get Spike Lee and Flip Wilson! Lee, the American director of uncompromising films about black urban life, famed for his ceaseless heckling as owner of courtside season tickets to Knicks basketball games at Madison Square Garden, concocted a series of spots using a stationary camera to film Wilson, the 1960s TV relic, performing a nearly embarrassing caricature of a black Baptist preacher, singing the praises, say hallelujah! of the next playoff match-up.

Bizarre and uncomfortable-making were not the only terms that sprang to mind when these promos aired. You got the impression that Lee—who once professed that he had disliked hockey ever since he was a little boy, when a Ranger coach, in what Lee took to be a racially loaded superstitious gesture, rubbed Lee's head—was somehow employing minstrelsy to mock hockey for its whiteness. Ultimately, you had to wonder how two artists like Lee and Wilson, who aren't exactly steeped in the game, could be expected to speak to hockey's audience. But of course, the point wasn't to encourage hockey fans to watch, it was to get people who *don't* like hockey to watch—although we doubt that the sale of Rangers tickets in Fort Greene, Brooklyn, skyrocketed as a result of Lee's ads.

Over and over again, hockey fails to understand its loyal and knowledgeable core audience and relentlessly seeks to present the game as louder, bigger, simpler, meaner, flashier, dumber, in order to attract a new audience—an audience of sports fans who aren't hockey fans. What are those people watching instead? Just a guess, but we'd say that when the NHL is getting under way in September and October, they're following the pennant races and the league playoffs and the World Series in baseball; and when the NHL season starts taking shape from October through January, they're following college and pro basketball, and college and pro football, and college bowl games and the NFL playoffs and the Super Bowl; and when the NHL season actually starts heating up around March, they're watching the NBA season heat up and college basketball's NCAA tournament; and when the NHL division races are being decided in April, they're watching the NBA races being decided and baseball cranking up its new season—and when the NHL at long last gets around to the Stanley Cup Final sometime in June, they're watching the NBA finish up its own championship series and cleaning their grills for their Fourth of July barbecues.

But the NHL and American network television never arrive at the obvious conclusion that the season is just too damn long, and that it runs hockey up against the most immense and popular institutions on the American sports schedule; they're obsessed with the notion that hockey is too dull and too complicated and not enough like those other sports to capture the attention of the American sports public. So televised hockey is subjected to the worst treatment that TV directors with too many switches and computer gimmicks can crank out.

There's loads of glitzy window dressing, with animated cyberjunk framing our view of the game, and animated chrome-plated hockey equipment and cartoon robots slamming into each other and blowin' up real good with flames and shrapnel, and animated technojunk with animated buttons and touchpads churning out screens of pseudocomputerized stats and scouting reports complete with electronicized sound effects, and the animated cartoon robots again, gettin' down and gettin' jiggy wit' every instant replay and out-of-town update and commercial break, to draw the fleeting attention of the little kids.

There's continual switching back and forth from one bizarre camera angle to another, disruptive even to veteran viewers well able to follow the flow of play, let alone to the neophytes the NHL wants to recruit as fans. Each angle, more clever, artsy, and useless than the last: Here's the action seen from behind the net! Here's the action seen from the corner! Here's the action seen from the ceiling of the arena! Here's the action seen from the goalie's helmet! Here's a sudden zoom in to an extreme close-up of the defenceman's left eye! Hey, TV director... yeah *you*, Kubrick. *Who cares?* Put the camera halfway up the seats at centre ice and *leave* it there, so we can watch the damn game without needing Dramamine.

No worse than these offences, but certainly more infamous and every bit as annoying: of course, it's the Fox Trax glowpuck, now an endangered species, thank God. What can be said that hasn't already been said about the little blue electronic nimbus that rolls around the boards flickering like a flashlight with loose batteries and criss-crosses the ice leaving a stain of disappearing ink leaking behind it? It's distracting, it's hypnotic, it's infuriating—most of all it's insulting, because what it really says is this: Screw all the fans in the cities where they know and love hockey. Some drawling hick somewhere complained *he cain't foller that l'il ol' puck thang on the TV*, so the game is dumbed down about as far as it can go, short of having a representative from the NHL or Fox actually standing in the living room, continuously indicating where the puck is by using his finger to point to it on the screen.

Will the NHL not be satisfied until the game has been reduced to such bland uncomplicated pabulum that even the inbred hillbillies from *Deliverance* will be grinning and grunting in toothless enthusiasm? Is this the audience the NHL wants? How many marketing dollars do they expect to rake in from Kentucky cabins and Texas trailer parks? "The NHL," says Internet hockey writer Jim Iovino, "would rather have to explain every rule of the game from icing to cross-checking to a novice audience than cater to those who have supported the game for over 75 years. That isn't the way to say thanks. I think it's more of a slap in the face. 'Hey, we already got your money, step aside so we can get someone else's.'"

Don't the NHL and their TV buddies get it? Doesn't it say anything at all to them when the most wildly popular commercial involving hockey is the Molson ad featuring a southern-fried American TV marketing executive, standing beneath a portrait of Nels Stewart in a richly wood-panelled Canadian boardroom, pitching the virtues of the glow-puck and being regarded with such impatient contempt that he's thrown bodily out of the room and down the hallway? With a glowing red streak following his flight, of course. In bars where the game is playing on TV, people actually cheer when this ad comes on, and fists pump the air in joy when the guy is sent flying.

The clownish uniforms, the cartoon mascots, the dancing robots, the glowing pucks—they work. They do get the little children's attention. But do any of them notice the hockey, or remember it? Once they outgrow all the kiddie glitz, what's left to make them want to play or watch or care? Not much, if the league's U.S. TV ratings are to be believed. Between 1997 and 1998, the American male teenage audience watching NHL games dropped by nearly 40%.

Perhaps, in its yearnings for an audience of pubescent Sun Belt skate-boarders, the NHL's descent into the trappings of pre-adolescence is what has made it forget the lesson the rest of us learned by the time we were in high school: if someone's not interested in you, then no matter how much you want them, you cannot make them love you. And even if you do get their attention, if you do get their transitory interest and manage to persuade them to spend some time with you, the superficial solicitations you used to get them close for a moment are never nearly enough to hold them close for long.

The idea that hockey needs to be "sold," as anything besides what the game at its best already is, is so self-evidently wrong, it's just madden-ing. Is this a hockey game, or a birthday party for the kiddies at the Chuck E. Cheese Scrumpdillyicious Food & Funtime Pizza Emporium? Is this a hockey arena, or a suburban shopping galleria? Is anyone actu-ally still serious about the game that's supposed to be played here, or are sales of replica jerseys and nachos and team-logo earrings and wine coolers and little plastic mascot figures all that really matter now? All we want is two teams who hate each other, playing in a game that counts for something, in a building where we can get a couple of seats close enough to the ice that we can hear the players shout and hit, with-out having to pay a week's wages to get in. Because if we can't have that, we might as well all go to the West Edmonton Mall or the Mall of America and just watch the roller coaster go around. It would be about as exciting, all the franchise stores are there to sell us overpriced crap, and we can get in for free.

Chapter 5

bad blood

HOCKEY, ICE. The fastest of all team sports, ice hockey has been described as a combination of "blood, sweat, and beauty." With an increased focus on the bloodshed, descriptions of professional hockey games today are more likely to include words like "goon," "mayhem," and "degenerate." Stiffer penalties have not discouraged the players from using their basic equipment of sticks and skates as weapons, and this brutality has diminished the abstract beauty of the sport.

—Beginning of article on hockey in *Compton's Encyclopedia*, 1997 edition.

We've always wondered why, in all the newspaper and magazine articles about hockey and in all the hockey broadcasts on radio and TV, there is never any analysis about fighters beyond "He's tough" and "He won't back down if the other team takes liberties." There are a million articles on who the best scorers are, the best checkers, the best defensive defencemen, the best butterfly-style goalies, the best face-off men in the offensive zone, the best dressing-room leaders, but never anything on fighting, which is obviously a substantial part of every team's strategy. Why the blackout? We were thinking about this a few years ago, while

we were working on the sports section at *The Village Voice*, and we figured it would be a good idea to actually have a regular column about
hockey fighters in a regular newspaper. There were a few people at that
time doing hockey-fight zines, and we liked one done by a Chicagoan
named Mike Beaver, so in 1993 he was hired to do a twice-monthly column called "Mike Beaver's Mixin' It Up."

An unabashed admirer of the fistic glories of the ice game, Beaver
enthusiastically recapped the NHL's top fights of the previous fortnight
and pronounced on who the best enforcers were and why they were so
important to their teams. Hockey people would ask us why the *Voice* was
running "Mixin' It Up," and we would tell them: if fighting is *a part of
the game*, if general managers go to the trouble of finding and hiring
these players, if coaches put them on the ice at a particular time for a
particular purpose, and if thousands of fans go berserk when they start
fighting, why *shouldn't* we report on it? One time a league official came
up to one of us in the media lounge at Madison Square Garden and flat-
out asked, "Why do you print that garbage? Why do you give that guy a
forum?" We'd answer the NHL now as we answered then: if you don't
want that "garbage" written about, if you don't want to "give that guy a
forum," get rid of fighting.

This is an example of the profound cognitive dissonance between
what the NHL allows and what it doesn't like to see mentioned. What
does it mean when the league objects to a newspaper column about
hockey fighting while at the same time allowing the actual on-ice practice of fighting to continue? Does the NHL, as an institution, realize on
some level that fighting is something to be ashamed of, something that

should not be spoken about? It must; otherwise, why the huffy denials whenever fighting is brought up by the media?

Why *does* the National Hockey League allow fighting in its games? Why, when people make fun of the NHL and of hockey because of all the fighting in it, does the league let the fighting continue? Why does it permit its linesmen to stand back and *let 'em go*, then send these players off the ice for all of five minutes and wink knowingly when they step back on and do it all over again? The NHL has been fighting an uphill battle for some 30 years to be recognized in the United States as a full-fledged major league, a league whose goal it is to make money for its member teams. Yet it perpetuates exactly the one thing that most Americans say is ridiculous about hockey: fighting.

It. does. not. make. sense. Let's put the fighting hypothesis to the test. Let's say there's a fight in a basketball game. It happens occasionally. Do you hear people going around saying, "Whoa, that was a great scrap"? "The refs should've let 'em go"? "Boy, the Knicks really showed some heart last night"? Do newspaper columnists write articles *praising* the teams that got into the fights?

Short answer to all those questions: No. What *do* people say when basketball teams get into fights? *They say it's a disgrace, and that their sport is turning into hockey.* They don't mean this as a compliment. They mean it as the worst possible comparison they can make. They mean that hockey is something to be ridiculed, that the worst thing that could happen to their game is that it could become like hockey.

Here, listen. *New York Times* columnist Harvey Araton said it in 1993: "Forget for the moment the danger Anthony Mason, Greg Anthony, and John Starks present to opponents and to the integrity of the sport. If I were Patrick Ewing, and these hockey-imitating goons were threatening to ruin my first serious run for a ring, they would be on the locker room carpet to explain what they think they are doing." Another *Times* columnist, Ira Berkow, said it again in 1994: "Both teams ran onto the court, heaving punches, tackling one another and comporting themselves like hockey players.... The NBA, unlike the National Hockey League and the World Boxing Association, understands that its sport doesn't need fighting to survive. In fact, the sight of it on a basketball court is sickening." And Rick Fox, the Fox network's basketball analyst, said it on television in 1998: "It was disgraceful. We don't want the NBA to turn into hockey."

People abhor fighting in basketball. A basketball fight does not attract viewers; indeed, it might repel them, but we don't really know for sure because basketball fights are so rare that no one would ever tune in to a basketball game expecting to see a fight break out. So, are basketball's television ratings high, or low? We will answer this one for you, Mr. NHL Executive: Basketball's ratings are high. In the United States, they are four or five *times* higher than hockey's ratings. The NBA gets a huge amount of money from network television, several times higher than what the NHL gets, even with the hockey league's new contract, nearly three times bigger than the old one. Not only does basketball abhor fighting, the absence of fighting doesn't seem to be hurting basketball in the revenue department.

The NHL wants to make more money, right? The NHL wants to be more popular in the United States, right? But despite its growing "television footprint," the NHL has extremely low TV ratings in the United States; it gets relatively little coverage in most American newspapers; and people ridicule it because of all the fighting. Is it good to be the object of ridicule? Does hockey *like* being the object of ridicule? What, for Americans, is the most famous one-liner about hockey? "I went to the fights last night and a hockey game broke out." This is not the kind of attention you want your game to get.

And you there, reading this in Canada—why should you care whether Americans like hockey? Because of this naked financial fact: if all NHL owners, whether based in the United States or Canada, made more money from network TV contracts, there would be more money available for them to help keep Canadian teams where they are instead of moving them to Knoxville, Tallahassee, Honolulu, wherever. And like it or not, the big bucks are in big American TV contracts. That's how the NFL got so rich. That's how the NBA got so rich. That's how the Olympics got so rich. If the NHL wants to get rich—and we fans want it to because (a) it'll keep the Senators and Oilers and Flames and Sabres and all the other minnow teams in hockey country in business; (b) it may keep ticket prices in hockey, long the highest in any North American team sport, from rising any higher because the owners will finally have a more effective source of income than fleecing the poor suckers who actually attend games; and (c) hockey will at last become familiar to enough Americans so that we won't have to listen to any more Marv Albert sound-alikes explain what icing is *ever again*—if the NHL wants to get rich, it will do what it takes to make the game more popular in the United States. It will do what it takes to prevent hockey from being an object of ridicule. It will ban fighting. It will allow itself the chance to become popular.

Oh, right—we know what you're thinking right now. "But we aren't the ones who want fighting in hockey. It's *you* guys. You Yanks are the ones who like fighting. The only reason there's so much fighting in hockey is to sell the game to you Americans."

What a self-deluded claim that is. We know, because we used to believe it ourselves. We knew the drill: "Pure hockey, as it came south from Canada, was corrupted by American fans, whose understanding of the game was so limited that they only came to life when there was a fight. So, to sell tickets in American cities, the NHL encouraged fighting." Right. Like we say, we believed it. Until we went to our first game at Maple Leaf Gardens. We still remember it as if it were yesterday... yesterday... yesterday....

How wide-eyed we were as we entered the venerable building, rushing around the corridors trying to take in as much as possible. The portraits! There's King Clancy! Teeder Kennedy! Davey Keon! Squeezing through the narrow passageway to the standing-room section, packed with fans, into our seats in the old organ loft—having been directed there by some ancient usher from the days when streetcars were heated by little coal-burning ovens! The Gardens PA announcer with the effete, dulcet tones! And then the game itself, Leafs vs... well, the Capitals, but still! It was the Mirko Frycer era in Toronto, so there wasn't a whole lot to look at, but what a joy it was anyway. We kept a special eye on Brad Smith, because he was leading the Leafs in plus-minus, and besides, he was a fan favourite at the Gardens... because he fought a lot. He didn't that night; the Leafs had an uncharacteristically easy time of it, winning an 8-2 laugher that saw little physical play (it was Washington, remember). We lingered in this cathedral of Pure Canadian Hockey after the Three Stars were awarded, then stepped outside into the night. Several burly young fans in team jackets were excitedly talkin' hockey. None of the conversation, though, had anything to do with any of the eight goals the Leafs had scored. Instead, they were still enthusing over Brad Smith's last fight, from several nights earlier. "He totally pounded him!" "Smitty's the best, man. He shows so much heart!" "Jeez, his fists, eh? They're huge!" "It was righteous! He punched his lights out!"

It was with that magical experience that we realized the traditional Canadian line about hockey fighting is just so much malarkey, a fable Canadians tell themselves so they won't have to face the fact that they are responsible for making hockey the world's only team sport in which fighting does not result in immediate expulsion. But there's no way around it. Hockey is Canadian, born and bred; it did not leave Canada for a good 25 to 30 years after its birth, and right from the very start, there has been fighting and mayhem in it, long before the Mighty Ducks of Anaheim, long before Peter Puck, long before the Broad Street Bullies, who were all Canadians anyway, long before Eddie Shore, who was Canadian himself and used to make knuckle sandwiches in the Western Canadian Hockey League back in the days when electricity was still new to the Prairies, and we don't mean 1973. What's more, there isn't even anything about hockey that makes it imperative for people to fight; witness the entirely separate birth and development of European hockey, sans fisticuffs, in the late 19th and early 20th centuries.

No, the fact is that Canadian crowds like brawling just as much as American crowds. And we'll go one step further. There is no American amateur hockey league—high school, college, junior—that allows fighting, but the Canadian junior leagues do; in fact, fighting is actually taught in the CHL. Leaf crowds howled for Domi and Clark, and the allegedly ultrasophisticated Canadiens fans howl for Brashear as they did for Nilan and Ferguson and any number of *bleu, blanc, et rouge*-clad golems going all the way back to Sprague Cleghorn and Bad Joe Hall, so don't hand us any of this baloney about those tasteless American fans ruining the game with their bloodlust. Such as this offering in a 1998 article in *The Edmonton Sun*, quoting local playwright Ken Brown:

> Unlike Americans, Canadians don't go to the game to see a fight break out. 'We understand it on a deeper level [Brown said]. But if someone's playing dirty and screwing up the game, they better watch out because [a fighter] will straighten them out.' Brown regrets the Americanization of the game, though—especially when the Philadelphia Flyers overtook the Montreal Canadiens as the big hockey power. 'Hockey changed then from skill to violence. It marked a real shift in the game.'

Well, he's right about one thing, at least. But how the Flyers represent the Americanization of hockey is beyond us, unless the Flin Flon in which Bobby Clarke was born and raised was a secret U.S. base, and

Fred Shero, who devised the whole monstrous Flyer philosophy, was a stalking horse for the Fenians.

Even the perpetrators buy into the notion that it's the Americans who are really to blame for fighting, as evidenced by this 1998 gem from Sabres fist boy Rob Ray: "Look around this room. No one in Buffalo knows Vaclav Varada or Dixon Ward. The only ones who the fans recognize are Dominik Hasek, me, and Matt Barnaby. The players and a lot of the game in between go unnoticed."

Ray's a fine one to talk about the subtleties of the game. And if Vaclav Varada and Dixon Ward go around Buffalo unrecognized, well, there's a reason for that, and it has nothing to do with their unwillingness to fight.

The reality of Americans' reaction to fighting is a lot different than Canadian apologists like Brown and Ray would have us believe. The perfect distillation of that reaction came one night in *The New York Times* sports department, where one of us was working in 1997. The Rangers were on the television, playing some typically pointless midwinter game against some other Patrick Division—oops, sorry Mr. Bettman—Atlantic Division team. Predictably, as always happens under those circumstances, a fight broke out (at the game, not in the newsroom): Darren Langdon vs. what's-the-difference-who-it-was. Two or three hockey fans clustered around the TV to *watch 'em go*, when another sports editor, someone who had never evinced any dislike of or prejudice against hockey, wandered over to see what the fuss was about. This sports editor, an American, watched Langdon and his antagonist pound away at each other, then shook his head and muttered, "What a

sport." Then he walked away. He did not say it admiringly. He did not
say it in wonder. He said it dismissively. He could not take seriously any
sport that does nothing to stop its players from fighting beyond sending
them off for five minutes, a sport in which brawling and physical intim-
idation are recognized, tacitly encouraged strategies. You Canadians
don't know how many times we in the States have seen that kind of
reaction to hockey. The truth is, for every American fan who is drawn
to hockey because of fighting, one or two or more are repelled. As
Wayne Gretzky told Ken Dryden and Roy MacGregor in their book
Home Game: "We have such a poor image in California and the United
States, just because we allow fighting. We don't need it any more." So
much for the notion that fighting sells hockey in the United States.

It isn't just harebrained playwrights and fourth-line goons who
adhere to this idea. It has been generally recognized for years that owners, whether in big U.S. cities or in small Canadian junior hockey outposts, want fighting in the game, presumably to sell tickets on the
supposition that fighting draws fans. It is certainly true that at any point
in the game's 125 years of organized play, the owners of teams or directors of leagues could have done what every other team sport in the
world has done: expel fighters from games automatically, or, if they fight
persistently, expel them for several games at a time, or, finally, expel
them altogether.

But they have not. "Fighting is part of the game," so goes the cliché,
and the men who run hockey have seen to it that it stays part of the
game. NHL teams make high draft choices out of junior players who roll
up absurd penalty-minute totals (our favourite of the decade: Kerry

Toporowski, chosen in the third round by San Jose in 1991 after accumulating 11 goals, 16 assists, and 505 penalty minutes in just 65 Western League games). At training camp, rookies and players on the bubble stage a veritable Grand Guignol of please-hire-me mayhem, clubbing and thrashing each other in an effort to convince coaches that they'd do anything, kill or be killed, for the team. General managers always make sure they have on their roster at least a couple of goons—excuse us: "enforcers," "policemen"—and three or four more honing their pummelling skills in the minors. Should one get injured, usually because his leg snapped while being wrestled rinkward or perhaps because of a concussion incurred when his head smashed against the ice while he was falling, semiconscious, from a roundhouse punch that may also have fractured an orbital-socket bone as well as the hand of the man delivering the blow, they'll trade for another. It doesn't much matter, they're all interchangeable.

Throughout the regular season, coaches put out their goon lines whenever the spirit moves them, usually at the end of one-sided games so they can *send a message* for the next time they meet. And the league's goons mount an informal tournament—Domi vs. Probert, Twist vs. McCarthy, Ray vs. Grimson, Grimson vs. Domi, Probert vs. Twist, McCarthy vs. Ray, etc., etc.—to unofficially crown the league's hardest hard man. Then the playoffs roll around, games suddenly matter, and all the fighting stops. But don't worry, training camp is just two months away, and it can all start over again.

This has been the reality in the NHL for generations. Its own managers, coaches, and players use fighting as a tactic, and the league, despite periodic drives to temper the practice, never outlaws it. The NHL inserted its first rule specifically to penalize the act of fighting in 1922 (although there had been actual on-ice fights since the dawn of the game), and, since 1937, it has added to and revised the rule 38 times. But all those revisions have amounted to little more than cosmetic changes designed merely to put a lid on fighting's more burlesque features. The revising really picked up steam in the 1970s, when every dust-up, no matter how pedestrian, triggered a clearing of the benches. Those were great fun to watch, but games started stretching a full 45 minutes longer, unduly delaying the start time of CTV's "Pig and Whistle" reruns, so a rule was introduced: The first man over the boards gets a game misconduct. Then, three fights in the same game and you get an automatic game misconduct (think about it: three fights in one game—*now that's going a little too far, son*). A few years later: The third man to join a fight already in progress gets automatically thrown out. Then, into the 1980s, if you fight with tape on your hands, you get automatically thrown out. Then, a few years later: If you're wearing a visor and you get into a fight, you get automatically thrown out *unless you take off your helmet first*. (This is starting to sound like a list of rules drawn up by a wacko banana-republic dictator in an early Woody Allen film: From now on, the official language will be *Swedish*; everyone must change their underwear *twice a day*; underwear will be worn on the *outside*, so we can *check...*).

Then, in the 1990s: if a fight breaks out, everyone else has to retreat to the neutral zone or else they get automatically thrown out. Next: if you get into a fight and your entire shirt and upper-body gear come off and free you up to swing unencumbered, you get automatically thrown out. This last one was occasioned by complaints from hockey people about our old friend Ray; he'd concocted the devilish ploy of tying his sweater to all his upper-body pads, so that as soon as someone grabbed his shirt in anger everything would come off and a bare-chested Razor would thrash his foe. One time in the mid-1990s Ray pulled this gambit against a Ranger, and John Davidson, doing the telecast for the Madison Square Garden network, where he could safely drop the objectivity he affects for Fox and CBC, was appalled. "That's not right!" he shouted. "*It's not manly!*" J.D. continued to splutter in high dudgeon as Ray strutted around the ice bare-torsoed, like the Charlestown Chief doing the striptease at the end of *Slapshot*. "There ought to be a rule against that kind of garbage!" The NHL agreed. Two grown men punching each other in the middle of a game is one thing, but someone taking his shirt off in order to get in an extra punch, whoa, that's just not right.

At any point the league could have just ruled that fighting, per se, is illegal, but it has performed a prolonged series of moral contortions instead, allegedly to "control" the practice but really to preserve it in the face of ever more obvious evidence that it is plainly ridiculous. Because, supposedly, fighting draws fans.

So, if fighting is a real, time-honoured tactic employed by all teams and if its underlying bonus agenda is that it attracts the fans, why doesn't the league acknowledge that it exists? Do you ever wonder why, in all those promos that the NHL does for itself on television, promos that celebrate the rugged, bone-jarring elements of the game, you never see a video of a fight? Do you ever wonder why, when you buy a book written under NHL auspices or endorsed in some way by the NHL, you never see any pictures of a fight? Do you ever wonder why no officer of the league ever talks publicly about a player's fighting skills, the same skills for which 50 to 75 players are drafted, hired, and traded each season? Because—and you may not know this, but it is true—the NHL has a gag order that specifically prohibits any mention of fighting in any of its products, videos, or publications. We have run into this very order a few times over the years, because like most people who write about hockey for publication, at some point you wind up working on something that bears the league's imprimatur. It's not like you sign a contract or anything that says "Author(s) will refrain from including any references to 'fisticuffs,' 'donnybrooks,' 'battles royal,' etc.," but if you do refer to fisticuffs, some midlevel league personage will tell you, politely but firmly, that you can't really talk about fighting, and you really, really can't have any pictures that show fighting.

Does this strike you as odd? The thing that supposedly puts fannies in seats, that supposedly sells the game in the United States, is the thing-which-you-cannot-mention. Wouldn't it make sense for the league to talk up something that draws fans? The league will talk about injuries. It will talk about tripping and obstruction and high-sticking. But it will not talk about fighting—it's as though it doesn't exist—even though fights happen every night of the regular season, in full view of 20,000 people in the stands and millions of TV viewers. It's positively Orwellian, like the Soviets not reporting air disasters despite piles of smoking wreckage and hundreds of grieving relatives. Right down the memory hole any reference to fighting goes, because Big Brother knows that it's an absurd, repellent practice, but so what? Sure you saw those two guys fighting. *But you didn't see it.* Sure it happened. *But it didn't happen*—we don't remember it. And how dare you sell fight videos in *The Hockey News* classifieds.

You might think we were always opposed to fighting. But that isn't so. Some of our favourite hockey memories are fights. We're Sabres fans, so for both of us one of the best episodes of all time, and maybe the high-water mark in Sabres history, was the night in 1973 when Jim Schoenfeld whupped the Bruins singlehandedly. The young "All Along the Watchtower"-strumming defenceman tangled with Bobby Orr, pounding him to the ice next to the benches, but only after he had set the tone for the entire evening by drilling Wayne Cashman into the boards, crashing right through the Zamboni doors and into the tunnel, where they continued to flail away at each other as the Aud faithful sent up a frenzied roar. Schoeny drubbed them both and by extension the entire team, those strutting, preening, big, bad Bruins, all of 'em given a heaping, helping dose of their own medicine, not one of 'em a match for our guy. The Sabres were sparked to their first-ever win over the Bruins, and by a humiliating 7-3, yet. Then there was Game 7 of the 1983 quarterfinal series, the Bruins again, when Barry Pederson had been acting like a jerk all through the game, running Sabres, slashing them dangerously, throwing late hits on icing calls. This last was too much for Buffalo's big-hearted but normally pacific defenceman Mike Ramsey. He'd had enough, and besides, the flagging Sabres needed a lift, so he just dropped the gloves and challenged the Boston centreman. They went at it furiously in that rarest of fights, one inspired by real anger and emotion instead of by contrived posing. As he went to the penalty box, Ramsey was yelling fiery encouragement through his play-off beard to his teammates, and damned if it didn't almost work. Pederson behaved himself for the rest of the game, and the Sabres, over-matched and sucking wind badly, lasted well into overtime before finally succumbing.

And then there was the first Domi-Probert fight, in New York in 1991. Domi, only recently called up from the minors, squaring off against the dreadnought Red Wing Probert during a general free-for-all that had already made the Garden crowd a marvellous howling cauldron of hate. They fought and fought and fought amid an ear-splitting roar of primal frenzy, as if two jumbo jets were gunning their engines full throttle into the building, and still they fought some more, and when they were finally finished, Probert was a bloody mess and Domi was carrying an imaginary heavyweight belt over his head, that charismatic idiot grin of his visible to the highest rafter seats, where people were practically tumbling over the balcony railing with ecstatic animal delight. And then in 1992 there was Domi-Probert II. The anticipation before the game was literally unbearable, the Garden crowd, always depraved anyway, now out of its collective mind with bloodlust. Domi and Probert lined up for the opening face-off, and within 37 seconds they went. Again that jumbo-jet roar. This time it was Probert who thrashed Domi, pounding him again and again as if his very manhood were at stake, which in a sense it was, raining blow upon blow on the usurper who a year before had dared suggest that he, not Probert, was the heavyweight champion. The brain-addling roar desisted as Domi sank at last to the ice beneath Probert's vengeful fists. It was great, all of it. If they ever ban fighting, we're definitely going to miss moments like these. We'll miss all the euphemisms too: They want to tango! There's going to be fisticuffs! They've dropped the gloves, and here they go! A left! And a right! And another right! Look out! He lands a bomb! They're still going toe-to-toe! And finally the linesmen step in! That was quite an exchange of pleasantries!

See, we like fighting—it gives us a real charge. Over time, we've subscribed to all the rationalizations that fans use to defend fighting. There's what Ken Dryden, writing all the way back in 1983, aptly identified as the drive/discharge theory: the popular idea that if the players didn't fight, they'd do some real damage; *if they can't blow off all that steam with some good-natured brawling, they'll be using their sticks to cut out each other's eyes and livers!* Of course this theory, based on long-discredited Freudian notions on the therapeutic value of catharsis, is inane. As Dryden pointed out even then, psychologists had long known that behaviour repeated is behaviour learned, and acting out violence, therefore, only breeds the acting out of more violence. If the theory that one's aggressions are dissipated by indulging them in a supervised environment were an accurate one, then there wouldn't be so many contact-sport athletes arrested for assault and rape, and social workers would treat wife-beaters by having them spend hours slugging life-size mannequins of women. No, fighting in hockey games never made the game safer in any way; fisticuffs prevent nothing, and lead only to more fisticuffs.

We've also tried the no-one-ever-really-gets-hurt-in-a-hockey-fight rationalization, but of course this too is clearly nonsensical. Let's see, there's Steve Smith, Paul Baxter, Brad Dalgarno, Nick Kypreos, Cam Russell, all of whom suffered serious and sometimes gruesome injuries as the direct result of a punch-up. But hey, if fighting weren't allowed, just imagine the awful injuries they would have gotten, um, instead.

Then we went with the leniency plea, that Canada isn't a violent society, so that fighting in hockey is really somehow all right. "How can you be upset with our lone expression of violence, eh?" We realized this argument wasn't going anywhere when a friend of ours, watching a set-to on a TV at a bar, snorted dismissively, pronounced hockey ludicrous, and called for the channel to be changed to something else. We countered with "Well, it's better than bombing some Third World country, like we Americans do," but were met with baffled glances and the furtive eyeing of exits.

We even turned to the speed-metal headbanger rationale for a while—"Hey, we're lusty manly outlaw men! We can't be tamed!"—anticipating the NHL's own marketing of itself, but just how popular is speed metal anyway, and who over the age of 25 doesn't look asinine violently nodding his head to the rhythms of Slayer against the backdrop of "Don Cherry's Rock 'Em Sock 'Em Hits Vol. XXIII"? On the other hand, Ted Lindsay used to get into fights at age 39, but that's hardly an advertisement for the game, is it?

Even now we're torn. It used to be that fights were honest outgrowths of emotion, as in the Ramsey-Pederson bout we loved so much. But in the 1970s, the Flyer-ignited rise in goonery soon had thugs attacking skilled players all over the ice; no one, except maybe Jean Ratelle, was safe. Eventually, the fighting thing evolved into an entrenched, premeditated, goon-vs.-goon kabuki ritual. Nowadays, with the only fights, really, occurring between guys who love to fight and whose only job it is to fight, it doesn't bother us in the way that some lumbering yob mugging some Lady Byng candidate did. We almost look forward to them, and we usually enjoy them. We're not proud of that, but we've got to be honest. And if that's the solution to what we would really call goonism—the Schultz/Dornhoefer style of sucker-punching some tiny, skilful noncombatant with no provocation other than the fact that the victim is small, skilful, and unwilling to fight—then we think the current goon-vs.-goon ritual is an improvement. Not a good thing, we hasten to point out, but an improvement.

But that's just us, and a lot of other current fans. But not all. The wife of the one of us who's still married, and there's really no delicate way of saying that, but anyway, although she has become quite a hockey fan, and likes action movies whar stuff blows up real good, and complains as we do that the bad guy didn't die horribly enough, she will not watch fighting in hockey. She will go to the concession stand or hide her face behind the program at the game, or go to the kitchen or bury her nose in her magazine if we watch on TV, and shake her head at us as we grin when Razor waxes some butthead goon for the other team who was taking liberties with our smaller players. What can we say? Beth is a wise and tasteful woman, more intelligent and mature than we are. Oh!! Here they go again!! GO, Razor! OH!! Boughner's got a guy now! Boogie!! Pound 'im!! OW!! The Boogie Man! Now they're *all* into it!

Lookit Barnaby! He's jawing away! They're gonna go, you know it! We gotta take a break here so we can tape this....

We're back, in our shame. Shame, because as much as we enjoy the guilty pleasures of the hockey fight, now we have to think about the boy one of us has, age eight as we write this. He's a huge hockey fan, and he likes playing too, though he plays mostly on in-line skates in an asphalt playground under adult supervision. The one of us who's his father, and there's no delicate way of saying that, either, but the one of us who's his father is really happy that he loves the game so much, and that he already knows so much about Rocket Richard, Gordie Howe, the Summit Series and Ooh Ahh Sabres on the Golf Course, more than just about any eight-year-old American knows about hockey. We want him to play, and enjoy it, and hopefully to play well and have fun—but if he does keep playing, what happens at the all-but-inevitable time when he has to fight? He's good-natured, never the type to become a goon or a fighter, so what happens when some jerk cross-checks him and sneers, "What are you going to *do* about it?" Do we want to see him fight? Do we want to see him take that crap? What kind of choice is that? It's the choice that hockey offers, and it sucks.

At times like that, a parent sees the advantage of soccer, a game where sportsmanship and good behaviour are preached, where anyone behaving even remotely like a goon is summarily tossed out—that, we suspect, is a big reason why so many Canadian boys are now turning to soccer rather than hockey. But when you think about fighting and hockey in the context of your children, the Big Lie stands exposed, and you can almost see the wheels spinning upstairs in the mind of the apologist as he wrestles with the naked truth, that fighting is ugly, not something he wants his child to see, to learn, to adopt as a practice. Tie Domi once told us of how he has a tough time explaining it to his young children whenever they see one of his fights replayed on TV. "It's not something I'm proud of," he said, obviously unable to rationalize the contradiction. "It's not something I want my kids to see." Perhaps not, but Domi keeps on fighting, perfectly willing to sock someone silly with those cement fists of his, yet at the same moment laying off when the other man's head hits the ice with a crack. By the same token, the inability to justify his fist fights to his own children is what transformed Stan Mikita overnight from *le petit diable*, a provoked-at-a-glance madman, to a two-time Lady Byng winner. One night his son had asked him why he fought so much, and when Mikita couldn't answer, he vowed never to fight again.

Big lie or no, dyed-in-the-wool fans like ourselves won't abandon our love for the game when the gloves come off; we guess we're part of the problem. We despise the other team's goons, but kind of like our team's goons. And when the lads mix it up on the ice, we stand up and watch like everybody else. The only other sensation like the one you get at a game where, say, Domi and Probert go at it is the one you get watching "Jerry Springer." You just know they're gonna go! They're eyeing one another! And now... *Here's the woman who slept with your mother!* Whoa! *Baboom!*

This kind of stuff will appeal to some of your hard-core fans, like us, and it may not completely drive away some other fans, like Beth. But what about all the people you're supposed to win over? Are they going to start watching? And if you think the hockey-"Jerry Springer" analogy is a reach, read this March 1998 item from the metro section, not the sports section, mind you, of *The New York Times*: "Oddly enough, ice hockey, a sport nearly as violent as Jerry Springer's talk show, calmly accepts the idea that two teams can tie."

Note the casual, throwaway use of hockey as a synonym for violence. This is what hockey means in the United States; it is never presented as a metaphor for gracefulness, or excitement, or passion, or even for speed; just violence. After 75 years of NHL hockey in the United States, all most Americans know about the game is that this is the one in which thuggish players are allowed, even encouraged, to fight with one another. It turns them off, it makes them equate hockey with pro wrestling, roller derby, a marginal circus freak show. It makes "Jerry Springer" staffers like Henry Schleiff, the studio executive in charge of the show, look to the NHL for spiritual kinship, as in this April 8, 1998, *Times* story: "As Mr. Springer has done, Mr. Schleiff defended the show as merely a mirror of a portion of society. 'To criticize the messenger for this portion of society is fallacious,' he said. 'You might as well criticize the National Hockey League.'"

Well, yeah. You might as well criticize the National Hockey League. Criticize it for allowing our sport to look buffoonish, for cheapening it, for allowing it to be the object of withering ridicule. But wait—what's this? A glimmer of hope? The NHL finally did broach the topic of fighting, and in what seemed an encouraging way, during the brief off-season in the summer of 1998 (you remember: the week between the Red

Wings' Cup victory and the opening of training camps). The league hired Colin Campbell to replace Brian Burke as its director of hockey operations, and Campbell made headlines by saying he might recommend a ban on fighting. Could an enlightened volte face impend?

Not so fast. Turns out this is Campbell's plan for banning fighting, as recounted by the *Globe and Mail*:

> "Maybe if you only allow 17 players [excluding goalies] to dress [instead of 18], you'd eliminate the fighters," Campbell said. "You'd have to keep the good goal scorers out there. You wouldn't drop your finesse players and keep your tough guys, I don't think. So maybe dropping the roster is the way to go. Then again, maybe that's not possible. I'm sure the NHL Players Association wouldn't be thrilled about the idea of eliminating jobs. But maybe there can be a trade-off with the players' association."

Right. The way to ban fighting isn't to ban fighting, it's to drop a roster place in the hope that teams will voluntarily lose a fighter, and lose the other two or three hooligans each team carries to boot. But then again the players' association might not go for it. So maybe we should forget the whole thing and all just go to lunch.

Sounds to us like business as usual at the NHL, addressing a major problem with a minor, off-the-point rule change, like a surgeon treating a defective heart valve by bandaging a toe. But we should give Campbell a chance. Upon being hired, he did say that he wanted to speak often with reporters, players, and coaches about rules, officiating, and other on-ice concerns, and it would be an admirable change of pace for the league to seek opinion from both within and without (although he said nothing about speaking with fans; why is that considered such an unthinkable idea?).

One other constituency group that ought to be questioned about fighting and violence in general is the NHL Players Association itself. The players' union has remained resolutely silent on the issue for as long as it has existed—a baffling response, considering that so many of its members have been rendered unable to work through the careless violence of fellow members. The players we mentioned above who suffered serious, career-shortening injuries through fighting—wouldn't the union that represents these players have something to say on that subject? And what of the NHLPA's silence on other incidents in which careless or vicious behaviour threatened, cut short, or ended the careers of its dues-paying members? Why was the union silent when Gary Suter cross-checked an unsuspecting Paul Kariya in the head just before the 1998 Olympic break, or when Dale Hunter ran an unsuspecting Pierre Turgeon from behind while Turgeon was celebrating a goal in the 1993 playoffs, or when Ulf Samuelsson ruined Cam Neely's leg with a submarine hit in 1991, or when Domi knocked Russell unconscious, and so on and so on? The union's silence on these matters makes it complicit in the violence, complicit in the harm done to its own members.

A sports players' union does not have to behave this way, as an example from the 1998 soccer World Cup illustrates. Before a free kick in the tournament semifinal, Croatia's Slaven Bilic grabbed France's Laurent Blanc, and, when Blanc softly pushed him away, Bilic crumpled to the ground, clutching his forehead and feigning agony. The referee was fooled. He red-carded Blanc, which meant not only that Blanc was ejected and that France would have to play a man down for the rest of the game, but also that Blanc would be ineligible to play in the World Cup final. It was a dirty trick Bilic pulled, the kind of skulduggery that happens all too often in soccer, but under the circumstances this particular piece of gamesmanship had gone beyond the pale—so much so that Bilic, guilt-ridden, tried to apologize to Blanc after the game. The next day the deputy chief executive of Bilic's union, the Professional Footballers' Association in England (at the time, Bilic played his club soccer for Everton in the English Premier League), spoke out against what Bilic had done. "It's sad to think," said the PFA official, Brendan Batson, himself a former player, "that the actions of one professional can get another professional possibly cautioned or sent off, and now Blanc will miss the most important game there is." What made the union official's statement all the more remarkable was that the offended party in this instance, Blanc, played his club soccer in France and was not a member of the PFA.

It is inconceivable that the NHLPA, when confronted with a similar situation, would speak out in favour of what's right. Its players drop like infantrymen at Ypres from high sticks, low-bridge submarine checks, bare-knuckle sucker punches, blindside charges into the boards, spears to the groin, and two-handed slashes across forearms, wrists, knees, and ankles, and the union says nothing and does nothing.

Like the NHL owners and league officials, the players' association is silent about fighting and violence in hockey, despite all the harm it does the game on the ice, despite all it does to marginalize the game in the

United States and, by extension, keep profits down, despite all the evidence that Europeans who grow up playing a far less violent brand of hockey have become better players than North Americans. It is a harmful, limiting policy the NHL is pursuing by continuing to preserve fighting, a policy that has failed at every turn. It has left hockey a laughingstock, the buffoon of team sports.

Chapter 6

empire of the suits

I reject the notion this is a game in trouble. On the contrary, I think the vital signs are good. We have strong ownership and the franchises have never been more stable.

—Gary Bettman, speaking at a press conference, June 1998

So hockey's a mess now. On that we're all pretty much in agreement. Unless you're younger than, say, nine years old, or are still suffering from the effects of a severe concussion, your list of the best things in hockey, like ours, would not include items like "cartoon robots," or "the way the NHL season goes on into the middle of summer," or "lifeless, meaningless games," or "gigantic, sterile, high-tech stadiums with terrible sight lines," or "ostentatiously ugly uniforms with more colours than you can remember to name and crests that look like characters from a cheap Saturday-morning kids' show."

Yet these are the most obvious features of hockey in the 1990s. This is what much of the game has become. It's not by accident that things have turned this way. It's not through oversight. These are the things that the NHL itself encourages and uses in its counter-productive efforts to "improve" and promote the game. How did things get this way? Of course, it's always easy to point fingers and assign blame. That's right, it's easy—so let's do it!

It starts at the top. We're left with the disturbing but unshakeable sense that the NHL, and Commissioner Gary Bettman in particular, see their purpose as marketing the game rather than overseeing it, and that furthermore, they are trying to promote and market a game for which they themselves have not only a profound lack of appreciation, but an actual, genuine, deep-seated contempt—that the underlying attitude in the commissioner's office is something along the lines of "Let's take this drab, horrid, ridiculous old game and change it around at the most fundamental level, so that it's as cool as in-line hockey or arena football."

The unmistakable impression so many of us have of Bettman is that of a snippy, glorified accountant with an arrogant unwillingness to really know or appreciate the game at a fundamental level. He is in fact a sharp lawyer with a quick intelligence, but he has projected this negative image himself. For all his mollifying words about how the NHL would like to hold onto its Canadian teams and needs Canadian players, his actions speak more loudly. He has won points among the hockey media by having learned, at last, the difference between Bobby Baun and Bobby Orr, but you never get the sense he really understands it.

He has at least made the effort—he has learned some of the basic vocabulary of the game, rehearsed some phrases, and memorized some facts to make him sound conversant—but after more than five years in office, hockey is still not a language in which he is truly fluent. It seems as though the whole experience of hockey, the sensation of it, is still an alien culture to him. The ability to understand the game, to feel it and care about it the way you or we do as fans, to comprehend it as anything more than a multimillion-dollar ledger sheet of expansion fees and advertising contracts and marketing tie-ins and merchandising licences—that still seems well beyond him.

If Bettman were merely the NHL's marketing director or some such, this tone-deafness would be bad enough. But Bettman, who came to the NHL as a business and marketing guy from the National Basketball Association—godfather of the salary cap and major consultant to the NBA's property division—has made the game's finances and promotional strategies the NHL's major focus since he took over as commissioner. There's no objection at all from us—in principle—to his leaving the job of dealing with the on-ice aspects of the game to other, more experienced hockey people in the league's front office. They've often done a terrible job of it, but that's a separate issue. And no one can condemn the league for wanting to increase its visibility and its profitability; those, obviously, are good things for hockey and for us as fans. No, what's exasperating is that marketing seems to have replaced any concern for the game itself as the NHL's focus, and, beyond even that, the whole approach to marketing the game has been as bad, as wrongheaded, in its own clueless, overaggressive way during Bettman's regime as it was in its veritable non-existence during the Clarence Campbell and John Ziegler regimes that came before his.

You have to give Bettman this much: he certainly has more energy and integrity on his worst day than Campbell and Ziegler displayed in their combined 46 years in office. And he's trying to manage a league run by a group of owners as inept and unsavoury as you could find anywhere in sports: when these guys get together, it's not the Edwardian gentlemen's club of principled, avuncular sportsmen we'd all like to picture; it's more like that cartel of shadowy, malevolent billionaires who gather to manipulate global events in "The X-Files." Do these men have any love for anything about hockey except how much money they can wring out of it, and out of you and us, the fans? These are the skinflints with big cuff links and the faceless corporate automatons who cook up schemes like pay-per-view telecasts and personal seat licences, and who demand that your city tear down your team's terrific old rink and replace it with a billion-dollar "state-of-the-art facility" filled with luxury suites for other millionaires and corporate automatons, or else they'll move the team to a city that's willing to do all that for them. These are the men who have final say on expansion and schedules and rule proposals. These are the men who really run the NHL. Bettman is the man the owners picked to be their hired gun, but he's more than just their hired gun; he's also the one they look to for direction.

How is it that the league arrived at this point? The scenario, at least to all outward appearances, seemed to be this: NHL president John Ziegler, whose successes in his 15 years in office were infrequent and more the result of fortunate circumstance than forethought, and whose

failures were immense, continual, and obvious, is, for all practical purposes, ousted in 1992 by a Board of Governors freshly galvanized by the
forward-thinking if later criminally disgraced Bruce McNall. The NHL's
longtime chief legal counsel, Gil Stein, takes over as interim president,
providing a refreshingly accessible, knowledgeable, take-charge presence, but shoots himself in the foot apparently in committing the somehow unpardonable sin of arranging to have himself elected to the
Hockey Hall of Fame while still in office, the same honour gracelessly
afforded his two predecessors. Meanwhile, the NHL Players
Association, long misled and docile as lapdogs, has suddenly smartened
up and become a militant force. Stein, whom the owners regard as too
closely tied to the Campbell and Ziegler administrations, is brusquely
bypassed for the permanent position, as the governors, frightened by the
players' new assertiveness and dazzled by the way the once-stumbling
NBA has flown past the NHL in popularity and profitability, decide
that an NBA guy shall lead them. They hand the retitled office of commissioner to hockey virgin Bettman, the salary-cap wizard. Bettman
then convinces the goggle-eyed governors that in order for hockey to
make them even more money, the game must become more popular in
the States, and in order for it to be more popular in the States, everything about it has to be changed.

And this is where everything's gone wrong. For whatever reasons—
a total ignorance of the game's history and traditions, a complete inability to identify with the fans, a thoroughgoing lack of understanding of
what constitutes good hockey, or the misguided interpretations of marketing research focus groups—Bettman's administration jumped to the

conclusion that there was something inherently unsound in the game itself, that the game we've all loved for better, for worse, for richer or poorer, through all these years, was profoundly lacking in innate worth.

Bettman and the owners have proceeded on the basis of that presumption. Never do they seem to have considered that hockey's low standing in the hearts and minds of American sports spectators—at least the many of those outside of New England, the Great Lakes region, and Minnesota—might be due to the drastic watering down of the quality of the game through overexpansion during the Campbell years. Nor have they considered that it might be due to the bloody black eye hockey gave itself through inattention to the hyperviolence in the game late in Campbell's regime. Nor have they considered that it might be due to the failure of the league in the last two decades to take advantage of the promotional windfall it had on its hands with the simultaneous presence of Gretzky and Lemieux, two of the greatest and most exciting players in the game's history.

Whether Bettman and the owners ever actually examined the NHL's past blunders and merely dismissed them as factors, or whether none of those things ever even occurred to them, the NHL moved ahead without hesitation on the premise that hockey wasn't particularly popular in San Antonio and Orlando because the game was dull, its rules and strategies were dull, its look and style were dull, its history and customs were dull. And that belief is what is driving hockey today right into the ground.

The action itself, the images and memories, the history and heritage, the sights and sounds and sensations of our dull little game are what make it special. It's the disregard for those things, the dismissal and abandonment of them by the NHL, that have in fact turned the most exciting game on earth into the dismal morass of problems it is today.

The NHL owners can't see it. They can't figure it out. The league is radically overextended, its level of talent badly diluted—but rather than acting to stabilize and restore the game, they rush headlong into foolhardy plans to water the league down still further by adding even more expansion franchises. The game suffers from a deadly scoring drought, due to sloppy obstruction-filled play and the overapplication of technology—but rather than re-energizing the game by enforcing the rule book, the NHL Board of Governors ignores the wisdom it contains and tries to dream up hideous and inappropriate new rules to try to clear up the mess they've made.

Consider the notions that had been bandied about at the NHL's January 1998 winter meetings, as the league's brain trust wrestled with hockey's crisis situation. The very future of the game was and still is in the hands of men who were discussing not merely tinkering with the rules by nudging the blue lines closer together, but seriously considering absurd proposals like shootouts, abolishing all offside rules completely, changing from the time-honoured three periods to a football- and basketball-inspired four quarters, and even enlarging the size of the goal itself. We would venture that any owners or league executives who support proposals along these lines, who could *endorse* such ugly, outrageous nonsense, stamp themselves inarguably as an intellectually bankrupt crew who have no love for hockey, no understanding of it, and absolutely no place being in charge of the greatest game on earth. (You cannot imagine our relief and amazement when the NHL announced in summer

1998 its sensible decision to step up its crackdown on obstruction and define precise new limits on the dimensions of goaltending equipment.)

The NHL, though, regards these notions as part of a necessary evolution, as progress and success. Is it because Bettman, and especially the governors, driven in limousines and seated in luxury boxes, still have never experienced what it means to be a fan? Or have they, but are so devoid of any ability to absorb the experience on any aesthetic or emotional level that none of it registers? Or is it, in the end, just that none of it—not the sensations, not the history, not the passion, not the fans, not any sense of dignity or integrity, not even the game itself—matters to them, as long as there's another million to be made here or there?

Bettman and the NHL owners have to come to terms with what it is they're trying to sell. If you're running the candy concession and your product is being outsold by a competitor's popcorn, you don't drench your chocolate bars with salt and hot butter in order to compete; you've created a disgusting mess neither loyal chocolate lovers nor popcorn fans will touch. If you're producing a long-running, critically acclaimed television drama about doctors and lawyers and it's suddenly being outdrawn in the ratings by a variety show, you don't start adding slapstick and musical numbers to your drama; you've created a screwy mishmash neither loyal viewers nor variety fans will watch. And if you're running a sport full of excitement and beauty, of finesse and aggression, steeped in tradition and already possessing a loyal fan base, even if it's not making quite as many hundreds of millions of dollars for its owners as other sports are making, you don't let it degenerate into a turgid wrestling match, deprive it of its dignity by turning it into a goofy carnival midway game, ignore the fans who know and love and support the game, throw away all the things that have made the game great, and try to sell it as if it's some other sport entirely. You don't try to turn hockey into basketball, or roller hockey, or indoor soccer, or arena football, or any other damn thing. You wind up with something that's neither fish nor fowl, and while it may lure a few customers as an item in a cabinet of curiosities, they won't stick around long, and everyone who loved it for what it used to be will have long since turned away.

Hockey is hockey, and if its true audience is a little smaller than basketball's or football's or baseball's, well, so be it. Maybe it's just a measure of good taste. John Cheever never had as many readers as Jacqueline Susann did, the Barenaked Ladies don't sell as many records as Michael Bolton does, and coquille St. Jacques isn't as popular as macaroni and cheese. So what? *Titanic*, processed potato chips, "Beverly Hills 90210," Deion Sanders, Ronald Reagan... all hugely popular, all hugely profitable, all utterly awful. What's best and what's most popular aren't always on the same list no matter what the category. And nothing of quality is ever improved by copying something inferior to it. Should hockey be any different? Should it sell out, should it betray its history and its fans by trying to appeal to the lowest common denominator, by trying to become a more popular, more profitable, but far lesser game? That's where hockey is headed—and it's the owners, with Bettman at the head of the column, carrying a flag with a big dollar sign on it, who have led the game there.

We've been bashing Gary Bettman a lot for the NHL's shortcomings, but you know, it's not really his fault. The league has been inept for as long as we can remember, under John Ziegler and Clarence Campbell alike. The real power in the NHL for all these years—and, we'd have to conclude, the real source of ineptitude—has been its owners, who you have to agree are a pretty lame bunch.

Let's do a little mental exercise. Let's say it's the 1980s, and you're a spy from the NBA (this is not, repeat, not, a reference to Commissioner Bettman) whose mission it is to clear your main wintertime competitor, the NHL, out of the picture to pave the way for your league's grab for world dominance. What would you do to ensure that your league— which as recently as 1980 was a disorganized mess whose championship series was shown, on tape delay, on late-night network television— would continue to outstrip and overshadow hockey? First, you'd want the NHL to become as invisible as possible, and you'd probably do that by somehow getting it off America's television sets. Yes, but how?... Wait! The NHL owners do it for you: in 1988, they dump ESPN and take US$50 million to sign over television rights for three years to SportsChannel America, an amalgam of local cable carriers seen only here and there in the U.S., a network that basically does not exist. And lo, when American fans are able to catch a game (usually they have to pay extra to get SportsChannel, if it's available at all), they are generally treated to a bush-league production that is actually nothing more than a local telecast with a tarted-up corporate logo. By 1991-92, the arrangement is such a fiasco that a pathetic US$5.5 million is all SportsChannel can dig up to pay the NHL for one last year of TV rights.

An excellent start for our NBA spy. But now it's 1994, the Rangers have won the Cup, and everyone's talking about hockey. It's being touted as the Next Big Thing! Look, here's an article in *The Wall Street Journal* saying exactly that. And now there's a baseball strike, cancelling the World Series and souring fans on that sport, which they'd been souring on for a long time anyway—all this has left an unprecedented wideopen track for the charging NHL to increase its forward momentum. What to do? Got to derail that train before it really gets going. But wait! Not necessary! The NHL owners have done that for you again—they've locked the players out! In fact, that's why they brought Bettman in in the first place, to try for a salary cap, or at least to break the power of the NHL Players Association now that the players have gotten rid of their corrupt leadership. And yes, the owners' lockout blows the entire first half of the 1994-95 schedule! Now it's the NBA that has the wideopen track! And the NHL has inspired something of the bitterness among its fans that baseball fans feel towards their sport.

That was another lucky break for our NBA spy! But now there's a new threat on the horizon, especially now that the NBA is doing so well globally. It's the 1996 Stanley Cup playoffs, being carried by Fox and ESPN to not-bad ratings, and the NHL has a World Cup of hockey coming up! The league is dipping its toe back into international waters, and it might just show that it, like the NBA, has some bounce overseas. Our NBA spy is frightened: if the NHL's international promotional blitz is anything like the NBA's international promotional blitz, this could be trouble! He watches the NHL playoffs on Fox and ESPN, waiting for the NHL's free, prime-time promos, waiting for the league to hype its big international tournament, which starts in just two months' time.

There's a Catch Cup Fever promo for the Stanley Cup playoffs, which doesn't make a whole lot of sense, since that's what's on now anyway, but whatever. There's another Catch Cup Fever promo. Hoo boy, he's scared waiting for the promo for the big World Cup tournament... there's the same Catch Cup Fever promo. There it is again. And again. Where's the World Cup promo? Wait a minute, there's none! None at all! Could it be that the league will not say a single word to promote its big World Cup tournament? Last game of the Cup Final. Surely here... Catch Cup Fever. No World Cup promo! And sure enough, the World Cup will pass virtually unnoticed in the United States! So much for the NHL's effort to market itself as a global sport. Another triumph for our NBA spy!

But wait—the NHL's global threat is not completely thwarted. Our NBA spy shudders anew in 1998 when the NHL goes to Nagano for the Olympics. True, the games are on late, late at night; nevertheless, this could really propel the NHL into America's consciousness! The American women have done their bit, but that's okay, they're no threat to the NBA or even the WNBA. It's the men our spy is worried about and all that talk about the jubilation if the United States or Canada win the gold medal. But hold on... the Americans lose, and the league isn't doing damage control as all the commentators talk about the Olympic experiment being a failure. Bettman's in Nagano, being interviewed by Ron MacLean on CBC immediately after the U.S. is eliminated by the Czechs, and he's got a chance to spin it, to say that Americans ought to watch regardless of who wins, because hockey's a great game. But Bettman's sweating, he's wiggling and wriggling even more than usual!

Our NBA spy watches as MacLean asks the commissioner how much of a disappointment the U.S. loss is to the NHL's hopes for exposure, and Bettman nervously snaps at him, like Nathan Thurm, the shaky, chain-smoking, prevaricating lawyer Martin Short played on "SCTV". "It doesn't matter," says Bettman, a panicked grin on his face. "The U.S. doesn't need to win here to make our participation in the Olympics a success." Bettman has said just the right thing, even if no one believes him—but then he blurts out: "The last time I checked, our friends from Canada are still alive in this tournament, *thank you very much!*" He's tipped his hand! The United States *or Canada* have to win to make the NHL's participation in the Olympics a success! Otherwise, the whole thing's an expensive failure!

Then Canada loses too! And now what? A few Americans break a few chairs, and it's getting blown way out of proportion, and... yes! the NHL is remaining largely silent on the issue! And now the league is *joining* the chorus, demanding that the Americans identify themselves! The NHL isn't talking about how great the Czech triumph is! It's not shifting the focus away from this relatively minor furniture-trashing incident. It's letting everyone say the Olympics were a bust! And now it's making all kinds of demands of the organizers of the 2002 Olympics in Salt Lake City, demands about running the dressing rooms and playing on an NHL-size rink. Whew! Looks like the Olympic field will be left exclusively to the NBA once more. Our NBA spy is all aces yet again!

So it goes, as it always has gone: the NHL owners and the league office shoot themselves in the foot so consistently, so unfailingly, it's hard to believe they're not doing it deliberately. There's an old saying about the NHL: it's Murphy's league; everything it'll do, it'll do wrong—even when it's not the league's fault. Take the 1998 Sabres-Capitals semifinal. Game 3 at the MCI Center (um, that's the one in Washington), and who's there but Bill Clinton. The ESPN announcer, Gary Thorne, practically does somersaults of joy, pointing out that Clinton is the first U.S. president ever to attend an NHL game—making everyone who's listening wonder why it's taken until 1998 for a U.S. president to attend an NHL game. The president will fall in love with hockey, Thorne says, parroting the NHL's longstanding party line, because you've got to see it in person, it's so much better than on TV—which makes it sound like it's a waste of time to watch a game on TV. The president's going to love the intensity of a Stanley Cup game, he says; that'll make him a hockey fan for sure—but it turns out that he left the game before the start of overtime. The president will be back for the Cup Final, Thorne says, now that he's tasted the excitement of a live NHL game. The president never returned.

More often, though, things go wrong because they are mismanaged, or worse. And the effects can be devastating. Take, for instance, the owners' insistence on locking out the players before the 1994-95 season—perhaps the single most wrong-headedly counter-productive thing the owners have ever done. They wanted their salary cap—that's why they'd hired Bettman a year before—and nothing was going to stop them from getting it. General interest in hockey was at a 20-year high, the long sought-after U.S. television network contract was up and ready to go, and *baseball was on strike, leaving the sports pages wide open for the*

When NBA Senior VP and salary-cap guru Gary Bettman was being courted by the NHL to become its new commissioner, Pat Williams, GM of the Orlando Magic, said, "I gave Gary a hockey puck once, and he spent the rest of the day trying to open it." One of Bettman's big ideas for improving hockey was to replace the NHL crest with an NBA-style logo. We all want hockey to look more like basketball, don't we?

Every time the game begins to stabilize, the league goes on another expansion binge. Here Bettman poses with the owners of new teams from Atlanta, Nashville, Columbus, and Minneapolis, whose entry will bloat the NHL to thirty teams. No angel himself, even the legendary Conn Smythe once said, "Hockey must be a great game to survive the people who run it."

Until the last few years, goalies were still recognizable as humans inside their snug sweaters. Denis Herron and Eddie Giacomin were among the best, facing down the NHL's top shooters armed only with a typically thin shell of padding and gloves the size of oven mitts.

CREDIT: Canapress/C. Gardner

CREDIT: Canapress/G.J. Puskar

Every goalie of the '90s began to resemble the Michelin Man. As their equipment became enormous, so did their save percentages, and goalscoring shrivelled. Garth Snow and Ron Hextall, at a 1997 practice, looked like slabs on skates; trying to score on Patrick Lalime must have seemed like trying to shoot a puck past a building draped with an installation by Christo.

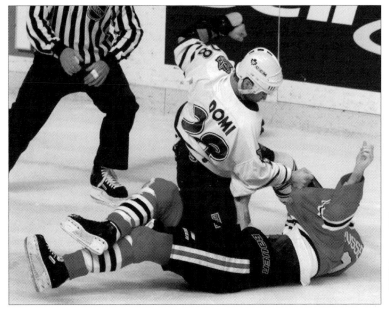

Critic Gary Deeb described hockey as "a sport of poetry and reckless adventure." Why should it have to degenerate into a caveman competition? Tie Domi is poised to deliver the *coup de grace* to the fallen Cam Russell; as Russell was already out cold with a severe concussion, Domi graciously declined. Lacking clown costumes and Nerf bats, Steve Shields and Garth Snow don goalie gear for a frenetic slapfight.

More invidious and damaging to the game is the constant clutching and grabbing, tackling and tripping that slows down the action and defines the average regular season game. Here, Todd Warriner takes Paul Kariya out of the play. Who wanted to see Kariya do anything exciting anyway? Lance Pitlick demonstrates the approved technique for "sustaining your check." A thrill a minute!

The great old arenas were the game's cathedrals—each one unique, full of history and character. We were packed into all kinds of weird and wonderful places close to the ice, and we could actually recognize the players and talk about the game. Remember the Roar! La Fierté Pour Toujours!

At the old Forum, fans could race for affordable standing-room space, ready to display home-made signs and banners. Once in place, they could actually hear the sound of the puck as it hit the boards—as well as each other talking.

The new Molson Centre is two-and-a-half times bigger than the old Forum. So what? The boards and the ice are plastered with advertising, and for the average fan, the game is a distant vision. Crank up the ear-splitting, canned music to make those people up there think they're being entertained!

CREDIT: Canapress/J. Bryksa

Feisty Winnipeg Jets fans mounted a spirited campaign to keep their team where it belonged, but in the end the NHL's accounting system prevailed and the Jets were packed off to Arizona. (Where's the sign that spells out R-E-V-E-N-U-E S-H-A-R-I-N-G?)

The one bright spot on the hockey scene is the development of international competition. Any number of national teams can win a major tournament now and the battle for supremacy produces some superb contests. Here 100,000 hockey-crazed Czechs celebrate their team's Cinderella victory over Russia, taking the gold medal in the 1998 Winter Olympics.

CREDIT: Canapress/M. Dolezal

NHL. The world was their oyster at last, but nope, the owners sent Bettman off on his mission. The commissioner and the lords of hockey were certain that whatever setbacks the lockout would entail, it would be worth it to keep salaries down—and what's more, they believed they'd have no trouble restoring the NHL to its bright, shining place on the threshold of glory. But in fact, the lockout—not a strike, it is important to remember, but a *management*-instigated work stoppage— alienated fans in Canada, who were disillusioned and sickened by the bickering on both sides of the negotiating table. In the United States the effect was different: it simply returned hockey to the invisibility from which it had just escaped.

Months were lost. Windows of opportunity closed. The fans, suspicious of the grievances held by millionaire players and as yet not fully aware of the depredations of years of unethical and often illegal Eagleson-NHL shenanigans, tended to side grudgingly with the owners. And the players' behaviour did not always help their own cause. The goodwill they earned by staging charity benefit games was undone by a series of intemperate remarks. Blackhawks defenceman Chris Chelios told a television interviewer, "If I was Gary Bettman, I'd be worried about my family or I'd be worried about my well-being. Some crazed fan or even a player might take it into his own hands and figure if they get him out of the way, this might get settled." Other players and some journalists explicitly criticized Bettman for being "a New York lawyer."

In the charged atmosphere of the labour dispute, that combination of vaguely threatening speculation and veiled references to Bettman's ethnicity and non-Canadianness gave the whole affair a faint but disturbing undertone of anti-Semitism—not a far-fetched impression given the casual anti-Jewish bigotry, so well documented in David Cruise and Alison Griffiths's *Net Worth*, that pervaded league management in the past.

Finally, in January, a settlement was hammered out. The owners got a face-saving salary cap... for rookies, and one that could be easily circumvented by bonuses and deferred payments. In public, the players complained that they got jobbed—and then went out and renewed the same contract twice in the subsequent three years. Players' salaries, which the owners were supposedly going to keep down by teaching the union a lesson, doubled within three years anyway. Worst of all, the NHL had missed its chance. It has gone back to being an obscure and distant fourth in the United States, its television ratings down, general interest down; even in Canada, there is lingering disgust with what happened in '95. Don't think some owners, too, aren't upset with the high salaries the lockout failed to prevent—and might eventually start looking at Bettman, their salary-cap guru, as a fall guy.

It must be said, though, that the NHL comedy of errors is hardly the exclusive production of the current regime. The leadership of the National Hockey League has been a three-ring circus since its very inception in 1917, when four of the five owners of the National Hockey Association decided to ostracize Toronto owner Eddie Livingstone with a back-door manoeuvre: they pulled out of the NHA, leaving Livingstone's Toronto team as its only member, and formed the NHL. Such are the league's noble beginnings. From there the parade of "colourful" executives marched on. League president Frank Calder dissolving the Hamilton Tigers and expelling them from the playoffs for daring to demand the post-season wages they were owed. The Tigers becoming the New York Americans, owned by future convicted boot-legger Bill Dwyer. The Norris family, targets of U.S. organized crime investigators, cornering the six-team NHL by owning three of the league's teams. League president Clarence Campbell, dignified public face of the NHL, convicted of trying to bribe a legislator to get a lease extension for an airport duty-free shop. Leafs co-owner Stafford Smythe charged with theft and fraud, his partner Harold Ballard going to jail on the same charges. Alan Eagleson, founder and leader of the players' union at the same time he was a close associate of the owners and orga-nizer of international competitions, convicted of defrauding the players' pension fund of millions of dollars. League president John Ziegler, at one time an object of investigation in the pension-fund case though never charged, but mysteriously absent for days during a league crisis involving a referees' walkout during the playoffs.

And then there's the "new blood": Kings owner and chairman of the board of governors Bruce McNall, boasting in a national magazine of smuggling antiquities out of Turkey and eventually being convicted of defrauding banks of millions of dollars. North Stars owner Norm Green moving his team to Dallas while at the same time facing a pending sexual-harassment case in Minnesota. All the way up to 1997, when the Islanders were bought by John Spano, a man with a vague financial past that the NHL did not find out about for months, until he missed his first couple million dollars' worth of payments, because the league's method of screening this potential owner consisted of paying $525 to a private detective, some $30,000 to $50,000 less than the NFL and Major League Baseball usually spend on standard background checks. Spano eventually pleaded guilty to charges of fraud. And, in April 1998, *The New York Times* revealed that no one in the league office had ever met Takashi Okubo, the shadowy Japanese owner of the ragtag Tampa Bay Lightning. "I've never said I had to meet him," Bettman told the *Times*, doing his best Nathan Thurm, "but I want to meet him." Four days after the article appeared, Bettman managed to meet with Okubo. A month later, the team was sold.

If you were being kind, you'd call this collection of grifters a "gallery of rogues," but the high percentage of convictions and jail terms suggests something different, a tradition of mismanagement and malfeasance that has stretched out over the entire 80-plus years of the league's existence. Small wonder it seems like there's no hand at the NHL tiller; how's the league going to manage mundane matters like schedule-making, or the clever spin if the Olympics go momentarily off-track, when it can't figure out whether someone who has spent US$165 million to buy a team actually has the money or not?

Given this history, should we really be surprised at the league's slow response when Sheldon Kennedy reveals the prevalence of sexual abuse in the already bizarre world of junior hockey, or when the scope and longevity of a child-sex ring at Maple Leafs Gardens is uncovered? Should we really be surprised when the league's response to a 1998 story in *Details* that points to the involvement of Russian NHLers with the Russian mafia is not to come down strongly against players consorting with crime figures as other leagues do, but rather to threaten to sue the magazine?

And should we really be surprised when the league, confronted with all the evidence of disgruntled fans and journalists on both sides of the border, falling television ratings, a dwindling presence in the culture at large, and derision when it does get the attention of the culture at large, denies that it has a problem at all? "A little fine-tuning" is all Bettman would admit the NHL needed when asked at the 1998 Cup Final about all the crises the league faced.

Stu Hackel, the NHL's director of communications until he was sacked when Bettman took over, may have summed it up best in an op-ed piece in *The New York Times*'s sports section during the 1998 Cup Final.

> When the present NHL regime came to power in 1993, they moved to "fix" the game and the business with an army of executives from other sports and fields. Their unspoken (and sometimes spoken) theme was that hockey people had made a mess of things and they were going to show how it was done.
>
> Their modernization has included a damaging lockout, an on-ice officials' strike, four franchise relocations, two realignments, a flattening of licensing growth, a merry-go-round of rule changes, an ill-conceived venture into the Winter Olympics [we vehemently disagree with Hackel on this point], unmanageably soaring salaries, escalating ticket prices, too many empty seats, the specter of four more diluting expansion franchises, lots of red ink, and now a drop in television viewership on both sides of the border.
>
> One trusts that these are all temporary conditions or problems of

growth, but if this were politics, an incumbent with that record might
have trouble getting reelected.

The NHL's staggeringly weak response to this damning indictment was simply to point out that Hackel had been "terminated" from his job five years before and might have an axe to grind. Presumably then, everyone who feels the way Hackel does, and that would amount to a couple of million people at the very least, are all peeved ex-employees.

Fact is, whether you're talking about the Bettman regime or any of the regimes that came before, it's surprising that the National Hockey League has survived this long, given the rampant and sometimes criminal mismanagement by the characters who have run it. But then again, given these characters, it's hardly surprising that after three-quarters of a century of operating teams in the United States, the league is still largely invisible in the majority of the country. And finally, given these characters, it's no surprise at all that the league has treated its fans with such contempt for so long.

Think of what you now have to endure to watch the game you love: outlandishly exorbitant ticket prices; months and months of virtually meaningless regular-season games; the destruction of intimate, tradition-rich rinks; their replacement with mall-like vanilla structures whose main function is to generate luxury-box revenue and put your seats a mile up in the rafters; the proliferation of "sales points" and "food courts" to fleece you by peddling overpriced junk; the high-decibel aural assault you must suffer with every visit to the rink; the diminishment of the quality of every team via runaway expansion; the cavalier tossing-off of the traditions you love via the "bringing up to date" of uniforms and the annual procession of pointless rule changes; the creation of a legion of new teams in cities you don't care about; the disappearance of teams from the cities you do care about; the liquidation of age-old rivalries to accommodate the gigantism of a league grown too unmanageably huge; hockey in June; the dumbing down of the game as a whole to teach it to yet another new generation of potential fans in distant hot-weather climes.

This is what the men who run hockey have done to the game you love. Are they fit to continue to run it this way without a peep of protest from us fans?

Chapter 7

lost in america

> In the Stanley Cup playoffs tonight, it's Washington vs. Ottawa. There's a bet on between President Clinton and, um, a politician up there. If the Senators win the series, President Clinton has to wear an Ottawa jersey, and if the Caps win it, the Canadian politician has to wear a Washington jersey. But there aren't many good stories going on in the NHL playoffs. I mean, there's the Caps-Senators series, there's Buffalo, can Dominik Hasek carry the Sabres to the Cup the way he carried his team in the Olympics, and other than that, what is there? There just aren't many things to talk about. Now the NBA, I could name 10, 12 good topics for discussion—there are a lot of good stories in the NBA. But in the NHL, two, maybe three stories, max. If there's anyone out there who wants to talk hockey, hey, give us a call.
>
> —Jay Mariucci, "One on One Sports Radio"

Or we could have started this chapter with another anecdote, one drawn from another U.S. talk-radio show broadcast about three weeks later in the spring of 1998. It would have been excerpted from the June 17 "Imus in the Morning," the daily show out of New York carried by more than 100 stations across the country. We would have recounted how the show's sportscaster began the sports update with an audio clip of play-by-play man Sam Rosen counting down the final seconds of the previous night's Stanley Cup game, before the clip was interrupted by the imperious host, Don Imus.

"What the hell is that?"

"It's the Detroit Red Wings."

"What'd *they* do?"

"They won the Stanley Cup last night."

"Oh."

As the sportscaster recapped Game 4 of the Wings' sweep, Imus proceeded to snore ostentatiously to the general hilarity of his on-air lackeys. Thus was the awarding of the Stanley Cup reported to the show's audience of 10 million Americans.

Of course, there's no great achievement in gaining the respect of American talk radio, where not only the name of the man who leads Canada is a mystery, but what you're supposed to *call* the man who leads Canada is a complete mystery as well. (President? Chief Governor? Omm, the Unspeakable?) But whatever, for gauging the lowest common denominator, U.S. talk radio can't be beat. And from the way it sounds, hockey even ain't even in the fraction. Even Chairman Chrétien knows that.

But why should it matter whether the average American Joe knows or cares about the awarding of the Stanley Cup? Why should it matter how hockey gets reported in the American news media? Here's why: Because so much of what we hockey fans are now suffering through is the result of the NHL's efforts to "sell" the game to Americans who don't know or care about it. That's the reason the Fox Network put that annoying little tail on the puck, why the league made no effort to stop the Minnesota North Stars, Quebec Nordiques, and Winnipeg Jets from moving to Dallas, Denver, and Phoenix, why it embraces the ill-advised presence of Nashville and some numinously vague locale in "Carolina;" why teams wear bizarre uniforms that look like the packaging for Mattel action figures, and why they're still playing hockey during the run-up to the summer solstice. We're enduring all these monstrosities so that the NHL can sell hockey to the U.S. media, so that they in turn can sell it to Joe Sixpack, and neither the U.S. media nor Joe Sixpack could care less.

Hockey has rarely impinged on the national consciousness in the States in any significant way, although now it seems to do so less than ever. We didn't used to mind: a hockey story would turn up now and then in *Life*, U.S. network television would once in a while have a story on an NHL team, or something like the 1980 Olympic victory would inspire a short-lived spate of wide interest in the game. But hockey by and large remained a cult sport, and that was okay with us; it was the coolest sports cult going, by far. Then again, it could become annoying, especially if you got away from the Canadian border. People would ask you your favourite sport, you would answer "Hockey!" and they would look at you funny. Or they'd say, "Oh, I didn't have you figured for a hockey fan," which meant they assumed any hockey fan would have both sets of knuckles dragging on the ground and an overhanging brow. (We have only one set of knuckles dragging on the ground.) Or you'd refer to things that you figured were common knowledge even for non-hockey fans and get blank looks in return, like the time one of us was coaching youth soccer, praised the four-year-old son of a man who happened to be a prime-time correspondent for ABC News by telling him that his son displayed the same sophistication around the net that

Mario Lemieux had at the same age, and got the reply, "Who's Mario Lemieux?" This from a prime-time network newsman, so you'd figure he'd know at least a *little* bit about stuff like that, but the name Mario Lemieux had never crossed his radar screen. It makes you feel like an immigrant in your own country.

And this, we think, is one of the things Canadians just don't get about hockey and the United States. The game is really in a black hole in the States. Take the summer day we arrived in Toronto just after the Americans' 1996 World Cup win over Canada. We met someone who launched into a little tirade about how you Americans think you're so great in hockey now that you've beaten Canada, and oh, you're all so proud now, but you know what? Our best 1,000 hockey players are miles better than your best 1,000 hockey players, so all you Americans are deluded if you think you're a better hockey-playing nation now. And we could only look at him and say, "No one in the States even *knows* we beat you guys in hockey. It got almost no coverage in the papers, it was on some tiny cable channel, and everyone's paying attention to the Olympics and baseball and football training camp now anyway." We would've gone on to say that we'd have been shocked if even one percent of the American public was aware that the United States was the new world champion of hockey, but we took pity on the poor man and changed the subject. "My, what a fascinating network of underground shopping concourses your fair city has," we said, or something like that.

Perhaps the reason for Canadians' exaggerated sense of the importance of hockey in the United States has something to do with the proximity of Buffalo to Toronto, the country's media capital. Buffalo is in many ways Canada's *maquiladora*, a sort of Tijuana of the north, the only American city of any size that is dwarfed by the economic and media influence of a nearby Canadian city. That, plus the fact that the Bills and Sabres are the city's only big-league teams, plus the Western New York region's substantial Six Nations population, have all combined to give it a sports sensibility unique for an American city—in fact, it's the sports sensibility of a Canadian city. It's profoundly dislocating to drive from New York, where the sports talk is all Yankees and Mets and Knicks and who the point guard of the Sacramento Kings is going to be, to Buffalo, where you switch on the radio and hear the top sports stories: the National Lacrosse League playoffs get under way tonight, the Calgary Flames are trading their back-up goalie, and the defenceman the Sabres have just called up from Rochester missed the 6 o'clock Greyhound and won't get in until 8:30. Then you switch over to a Canadian station and hear the Northern Ontario skip mulling the thorny question: Which is harder, the World Championships or the Brier? (We are not making this up.) There is no other place in the United States where you can hear any of these things discussed in public, except maybe Hockeytown USA, and you know where that is. So Torontonians, and by extension all Canadians influenced by the Toronto media, can be forgiven for thinking that hockey is something of a big deal in the United States.

But the reality is that it is not, despite all the glowing pucks, hollering John Madden-imitating commentators, six new divisions named after American regions (so E-Z to remember) and so on. Hockey in the United States seems even more obscure and marginalized than ever.

The league's efforts to grow the game south of the border may have worked insofar as plunking down a large number of teams in places where basketball and tractor pulls are the big arena sports, but in terms of getting the attention of the U.S. media, it is failing pretty dismally. All you need do to confirm this—besides scanning the sliding U.S. TV ratings, which were small enough to begin with, or listening to sports talk radio—is to look at the play hockey gets in the sports pages of the nation's newspapers. It is almost always, in the parlance of the ink-stained wretch, "buried"—that is, off the front page, deep inside the section, more often towards the bottom of a page with a shorter run and less of a photo than a typical football, baseball, or basketball story will get. There are fewer hockey articles, daily round-ups are usually confined to one-sentence summaries of the night's games, and a big hockey story of general interest, like Mario Lemieux's farewell tour, the exclusion of Mark Messier from Team Canada, or the junior-hockey sex-abuse scandal, might warrant only a wire-service brief, if it gets covered at all.

Our newspapering experience has pretty much been confined to New York City and, as far as dailies are concerned, mostly to the *Times*. But even there, where what goes on the front page of the sports section is given a great deal of consideration by many editors and where there is a genuine effort to make sure that hockey does not get shunted too often to the back, the NHL runs a poor fourth behind the other team sports. At the *Times*, as at the city's three other major dailies, certain stories are no-brainers to lead the sports section: the Super Bowl, a World Series game, Olympic figure skating, an NBA finals game, the Kentucky Derby, and a few other hardy perennials are all automatic choices, but a

Stanley Cup Final game is not, unless it's the game where the Cup itself is awarded. But the real litmus test of hockey's struggles to gain attention takes place on an average sports day, when there are no apocalyptic events in the offing. On such days, when the contenders are, say, a Jets off-season trade, a Knicks starter's X-rays revealing a minor injury that will keep him out a week, a Nets game in San Antonio, and a Rangers home game, the question is tossed back and forth: What do we lead with? What is the second lead story? Which story gets the big photo, which a little one, and which gets none at all? Which story gets thrown out later if something more important happens? Far more often than not, the Rangers story will not win the lead position against even such lightweight competition.

An object lesson in hockey's low standing in the pecking order in the American media capital was offered on March 30, 1998. The night before, the New Jersey Devils, first in the Eastern Conference, played the Dallas Stars, first in the Western Conference, in Dallas. Remember that for the *Times*, *Daily News*, and *Post*, the Devils are considered a local team. Now picture the coverage had it been the Knicks, Nets, Yankees, or Mets holding the No. 1 position in its conference or division, playing a late-season road game in the lair of the top team in the west. The coverage would have been massive: the day before, all three papers would have had at least one scene-setting preview article, and the next day's game report would have been accompanied by at least one sidebar and an offering from one of the paper's sports columnists. The whole thing would've gotten the lead position on the sports section of all three papers and a big photo or two to go along with it.

The Devils-Stars game, however, got only one article in the *Times*, on the fifth page of the sports section. Similarly, there was only one article deep inside both the *News* and *Post* sports sections. No previews, no sidebars, only small photos.

What's really upsetting is that the three papers' consensus in this case was probably right. No one cared about the Devils, who have about as small a following as any major-league team in North America (this is one place where we agree with Bettman; there's no way in hell the New York area should have three NHL teams). And the Dallas Stars? What do they mean to the average sports fan? They have no history, no tradition, no sense of rivalry with anyone, much less the New Jersey Devils; they are just one of a whole gaggle of teams that blow into the area once or twice a year, with no more than three or four players even an ardent hockey fan cares about. And what real justification was there for declaring an NHL regular-season game, even one at the end of March, important? Was it not one of 82 regular-season games for each team, played over six long months? Isn't the real hockey played in the playoffs anyway? After all, there was no mystery as to whether either team would make the playoffs, and if they got an extra home game for finishing high in the standings, so what?—home advantage means next to nothing in the post-season anyway. Naturally the *Times* didn't put the game out front for its 1.5 million readers, nor did the *News* or *Post* for the 1.5 million readers they reach.

How the New York papers play a story is more important than you might think. What the *Times* does is watched closely by the television networks, by the newsweeklies, and by other papers around the country,

and certainly when it comes to sports coverage, the *News* and *Post* are
enormously influential as well. And unless it's something extraordinary
like the Rangers getting to the Stanley Cup Final or the Czechs upsetting the Russians for the Olympic gold medal, none of these papers
plays hockey above football, basketball, baseball, or, increasingly, tennis
or golf.

This has all got to be extremely galling to the NHL, which relocated
its headquarters from Montreal to New York in 1992 for the express purpose of being in the pulsing heart of America's media capital. The NHL
offices on Sixth Avenue are about 10 blocks from the *Times*, about 20
from the *Daily News*, literally a three-minute walk from the *Post*, and a
stone's throw from *Time*, *Newsweek*, and from NBC, CBS, ABC, and
Fox. Yet the league has long been more or less ignored by most of these
organizations, and, as ratings plummet, it is getting paid still less attention. And if you think hockey gets lesser play in New York, think of the
kind of invisibility it has in the newspapers and on local TV in more
southern climes, where there aren't any teams that go back to 1926.
When the Capitals reached the 1998 Cup Final, *The Washington Post*,
which presumably had been covering hockey on a daily basis since the
team entered the league in 1974, ran an eight-page special section
introducing Washingtonians to icing, offside, the difference between a
five-minute penalty and a two-minute penalty, and all the other this-is-
hockey stuff you give to seven-year-olds unfamiliar with the sport. In
1997, when the Whalers were threatening to move to, well, we're still
not sure where it is, but somewhere in Carolina, the Raleigh *News and
Observer* ran a page of messages from local residents left in response to

the paper's call-in question "Do you want an NHL team to come to the Carolinas?" The majority of the responses were negative, pretty much encapsulated by "I'm from North Carolina. I've never seen a hockey game, I don't care about it, and I would not go to watch one if we had a team here." After a year of reporting on the Hurricanes, one of the *News and Observer*'s writers who covered the team and the public's apathetic response to it wrote a column declaring the whole idea of hockey in the Carolinas a dismal failure.

Apathy at the rink, however, is not the only consequence of hockey's deepening obscurity. Apathy towards hockey in the culture at large is a bigger problem. Whereas before the mid-'90s it was recognized as the fourth big-league sport in the United States and thus afforded some attention in the culture at large, since then it seems to have lost its place at the table. In the early '90s you could count on a movie with hockey in it to come out of Hollywood roughly every year: *Sudden Death*, a scene in *Lethal Weapon*, some wry references in *Wayne's World*, even a couple of scenes in a modest indie hit like *Clerks*, all confirmed that the game occupied a place in America's collective imagination. But how many films with a hockey scene have appeared since the mid-'90s? When two sports were melded to forge a comedy premise, *Happy Gilmore*, filmed in 1995, used hockey and golf. In 1998, it was *Baseketball*—the paradigm of what constitutes a hot sport has shifted, and it doesn't include hockey.

The situation is mirrored in journalistic or academic discussions of sports: in the mid- to late 1990s, hockey has virtually disappeared from the conversation. For example, crossover academic superstar Camille

Paglia, writing about the cultural implications of the World Cup of soccer in the Web magazine *Slate* in July 1998, observed, "While there is
increasing interest in the sport, reinforced by parental concerns about
the serious injuries and draining practice time of American football, it
will be decades before soccer can hope to challenge our triple-threat
hegemony of football, basketball and baseball, around which an elabo-
rate academic and media culture has grown." Note the utter absence of
hockey from Paglia's formulation of American sports and all the intellectual and cultural stuff that goes with American sports. Hockey was
just as absent from the picture when the venerable intellectual weekly
The Nation devoted its entire August 10, 1998, issue to sports. There
were 13 separate articles in that issue on sports, covering boxing, baseball, women's basketball, men's basketball, football, soccer, college
sports, religion in sports, stadium finance, Title IX, sportswriting—and
nothing on hockey, save a passing mention of the early-'70s Rangers by
the liberal warhorse Sidney Zion, but only in the much larger context
of the Giants, Yankees, and Knicks. Had either of these two examples
been written in, say, 1994, we'd bet our bottom loonie that hockey
would have been in the mix. But as both were written in 1998, they, like
so many scores of other discussions of sports in America in the late
1990s, contain no mention of hockey at all.

What chance does the NHL give itself to win the favour of the media
and the public, whether in the steamy hinterlands below the Mason-
Dixon line or in the big cities of the northeast, whether in intellectual
journals or in gross-out Hollywood comedies? You can blame
Americans' inattention on the rubbish that now passes for hockey on

the ice, of course, but there's another problem that seems as though it's going to be harder to fix. Just as every fan knows when the real hockey begins—with the playoffs—so do the people making the decisions in the media. And like ordinary fans, the honchos at daily editorial meetings and weekly assignment meetings around that time of year are discussing the NBA playoffs and baseball's opening day. So the NHL playoffs get diminished newspaper play and diminished TV ratings. And in a year like 1998, by the time the Stanley Cup Final has croaked in, the NBA finals are all over the TV and the papers, as is interleague baseball, which the Major Leagues cleverly started in order to grab a little juice for themselves. Each of these events on its own, and certainly all of them working together, are enough to bump a mid-June Stanley Cup out of the picture.

Teams need playoff games to make money; that's the NHL's biggest economic truism. An extra playoff game or two, supposedly, can make the difference between losing money and breaking even for the entire year, and an extra playoff round can put a team in the black. Is this really true? We'll never know. Pro sports teams are not in the habit of opening their books to anybody. But one thing is for sure: by lengthening its season and its playoffs, the NHL has put itself squarely in the shadow of other, stronger sports. In the United States, it will never get more than a small fraction of the attention football, basketball, and baseball get as long as it insists on going head to head with them. Individual clubs may make some money off the absurdly bloated regular-season and playoff schedules. But everybody is well aware that the real money lies with U.S. network television. And as long as fans recognize that regular-season NHL games are essentially meaningless and thus not worth watching on TV, and as long as the playoffs meander endlessly into June, the league will never get more than a fraction of the TV money other sports get.

Want proof of just how disastrous the NHL's television policy has been? The Fox Network's Saturday afternoon NHL telecasts, glowing pucks and all, drew a modest 2.0 rating in the U.S. in 1995. By 1998, it had dropped to a miserable 1.4. That's a 33 percent fall in three years, despite the addition of Carolina, Phoenix, and Denver to the league's "television footprint" in place of negligible or nonexistent U.S. TV markets in Hartford, Winnipeg, and Quebec. The network's 1998 All-Star Game telecast drew a 2.8 rating—on a Saturday night. That's the lowest prime-time rating for any network television program in *American history*. ESPN's cable telecasts have fared little better. Its NHL ratings slid 14 percent from '97 to '98, to a 0.7, even if ESPN2's held steady at an almost imperceptible 0.4. In the post-season, baseball, football, and basketball ratings traditionally quadruple in the U.S. The NHL's do not even double.

League executives have always made a point of stressing that no matter how small the NHL's television ratings may seem, the league has always drawn well among men aged 18 through 34—hockey's "core audience," and a coveted demographic for most advertisers. Nielsen Media Research revealed in August '98, however, that the NHL's ratings among the 18-34 males had dropped 41 percent since Fox's first year. For teenage males, the rating dropped from 1.3 to 0.8 from '97 to '98.

Meanwhile, with so many Canadian teams gone south, even the once mighty "Hockey Night in Canada" ratings are way down. The '97-'98 season was the first in several years in which the telecast averaged less than a million viewers. A bigger U.S. television footprint in exchange for a smaller Canadian one, yet viewership drops on both sides of the border. Marshall McLuhan the NHL owners are not.

These numbers illustrate nothing less than a catastrophe. They confirm every hunch hockey fans have had about what is happening to the NHL: that the game, despite being exported to the sunny hinterlands, is not catching on there; that the game's loyal fans are so turned off by hockey's current state, they're leaving in droves; and that even the youngsters couldn't care less anymore.

With the NHL's television ratings in free fall, ABC and ESPN's white-knight offer in August 1998 to pay US$600 million for five years of telecasts—over 2 1/2 times more than what Fox and ESPN had been paying—came as a complete shock, baffling TV columnists and business writers across the continent. That averages out to US$120 million a year for the NHL from U.S. national broadcast and cable television, as opposed to US$45 million a year under the Fox-ESPN deal—almost tripling the league's intake, despite its 33 percent ratings drop. Counterintuitive? You bet. But the real reason for the big cash windfall had nothing to do with any belief in the NHL's ability to bounce back from its problems and everything to do with the television war being fought between the Disney Corporation (owner of ABC and ESPN) and Rupert Murdoch's News Corp. (owner of Fox and Fox Cable). In 1998, Fox held the local cable rights to 19 of the NHL's 20 U.S. teams—including, even, to Disney's team, the Mighty Ducks of Anaheim.

Furthermore, News Corp., whose sports-television empire already controlled much of the airwaves in Britain, Australia, East Asia, and South America, was using Fox Cable to mount a nationwide challenge to Disney's coveted and profitable ESPN. The battle, therefore, was not really over the right to telecast NHL games, but was rather a sideshow in the much greater donnybrook between two gigantic multinational media empires for supremacy in the world's most lucrative sports market, the United States.

How much of a sideshow? Consider the August 1998 combined ABC-ESPN offer to the NHL: US$120 million a year. Now consider this: in January 1998, ABC and ESPN agreed to pay the NFL US$1.15 billion a year for television rights. That's billion with a "b," not quite 10 times more than the NHL offer. And that went on top of separate CBS and Fox deals with the NFL that brought the league's TV intake to US$17.6 billion over eight years. The NBA? In November 1997 it doubled its deal with NBC and Turner, signing a four-year deal worth US$2.6 billion, or US$650 million a year.

So, to compare again what these three leagues make annually in U.S. television revenue: the NFL, roughly US$75 million per team; the NBA, roughly US$22 million per team; the NHL, roughly US$5 million per team. And now consider this, if it wasn't for Michael Eisner riding in out of nowhere on his Disney horse with his US$600 million offer, the NHL would be getting a lot less U.S. TV money, maybe next to nothing at all. And who brought Eisner into the league? Not Gary Bettman, but Bettman's predecessor, Gil Stein, during his only year as NHL president.

So now we come back to the NHL owners, totalling up their profits in the short term by tacking on more games, more teams, more playoff rounds—but they will never make the really big bucks, because they have lowered the value of their "product" (their term, not ours) by manufacturing too much of it, and because they have placed it in an impossible-to-win competition with America's big sports. These are businessmen?

Once again, we have to remind our Canadian readers that it is crucially important for NHL clubs to succeed with the American media, so they can get a big U.S. TV contract that will provide healthy revenues for everyone to share. Not just because it would help keep clubs in small "markets" like Edmonton, Ottawa, and Buffalo and because it might put a lid on ticket prices, but just as important, because it might discourage runaway expansion.

Stein, for 20 years the NHL's chief legal counsel and for one year its president, summarizes expansion's real purpose nicely in his memoir *Power Plays: An Inside Look at the Big Business of the National Hockey League*: "Selling expansion franchises is a tried and true way to make quick up-front money." In a sport without U.S. TV money to distribute, the only way to get some bucks is simply to charge someone a fortune to join the gang. "In June 1997, the NHL... announced a new three-phase plan, expanding to Nashville in 1998, to Atlanta in 1999, and to St. Paul, Minnesota, and Columbus, Ohio, in 2000," notes Stein, pointing out that the expansion will "infuse US$320 million of added capital into the coffers of the existing NHL clubs, which will provide short-term relief from rising player costs."

Stein should know, having been present for several expansions. His tale of what happened in 1989 and 1990, when the league discussed and then set about expanding, is especially instructive. Stein reports that among the governors, then-Minnesota owner Gordon Gund was a lonely voice opposing expansion on the grounds that there were already too many shaky franchises, including his own. "We don't have the luxury of NBC and Turner Network deals, which will provide each NBA club with $9 million per year," Stein reports Gund as saying. "The difference in revenues between big-market and small-market teams must be addressed. It is being addressed in the NBA now—a committee has been formed to deal with it…. The key components of revenue are league-generated revenue, local cable and TV revenue, and local gate receipts. A meaningful way has to be found to share these revenue sources."

Stein calls Gund "the most prescient person in the room" and rhetorically asks, "But you didn't really think his plight would slow the governors' rush for the pot of expansion gold, did you?" Sure enough, the governors voted to accept expansion bids.

The league set US$50 million as the expansion fee. The following year, 1990, the governors heard presentations from Miami; Ottawa; San Diego; Hamilton; Orange County, California; and two each from Seattle and Tampa Bay. The various applicants paraded in and gave their pitches, touting all the great reasons why they should get an NHL team. But to the governors, it all came down to whether the applicant would pay a flat US$50 mil; any hesitation, any alternative proposal to pay less or even in instalments, and the application was kaput. At the end of the day, only two applicants had not balked about shelling out the full fee: Ottawa and Tampa Bay. "After what the governors had heard all day," remembers Stein, "it was becoming clear that was all it would take. Like in the old Groucho Marx TV show 'You Bet Your Life,' I could see the little duck pop into view and hear Groucho's voice, 'Say the magic words, win an expansion franchise.' And what were the magic words? 'We'll pay the $50 million!'"

That's what's it all about—a money grab. No league has expanded as often and as recklessly as the NHL in the last two decades. No league has watered itself down so drastically. That is because those other leagues, the NFL, NBA, and Major League Baseball, all have revenue to share from big U.S. TV contracts. And one of the reasons those leagues are so attractive to the TV networks and to TV audiences is because they are stable. Eight new teams are not being added every eight years, as the NHL has done, talent levels are not being diluted, and fans don't have the sense that the league is spinning out of control. When any of these conditions does begin to emerge—when, say, the Cleveland Browns become the Baltimore Ravens, or when the appearance of the Arizona Diamondbacks and Tampa Bay Devil Rays seems to thin out the baseball talent pool a bit more—there is a huge uproar among fans and commentators, and the league responds to reassure fans that there is a master plan that retains a vision of what is good for the sport. The league does not react by continuing to expand. It does not react to a franchise move by mouthing a few words of regret to the orphaned fans—it finds a way to reinstate the franchise in the bereft city, as the NFL did in Cleveland. But the NHL, by expanding and expanding because it does not have the TV dollars to distribute, merely lessens the chance that it will *ever* get TV dollars. Every television executive knows that there are way too many teams in the NHL, that it is impossible to have rivalries anymore, that there are not enough good players to go around, that the multiplication of franchises makes it mathematically impossible to have a compact, dramatic schedule—in short, that the expansion-drunk NHL has binged away most of the ingredients you need for a telegenic sport.

Until the league recognizes that its ruinous policies have held it back (and don't expect it to anytime soon; its leadership has repeatedly demonstrated a perversely stubborn refusal to brook any criticism), it will continue to expand, continue to draw low U.S. TV ratings, continue to warrant thin coverage in American papers. And talk-radio hosts will continue to snore, amid general hilarity, when sportscasters report the awarding of the greatest trophy in the world.

Chapter 8

Six or seven
solitudes

I am a great fan of Canadian hockey, and I do not believe it is
in trouble, as some people suggest. Hockey is getting like
soccer. At the World Cup of soccer, there are 15 teams who
can win it. Now, in hockey, there are maybe seven teams that
can win. It's not just Canada's game now, it's the world's game.

—Assistant coach Slava Lener of the Olympic
gold-medal-winning Czech national team

For all that is dismal about hockey today, for all the Tampa Bay
Lightnings, all the Continental Airlines Arenas and Stanley Cups in
June and linesmen standing around watching as two goons punch each
other out, for all the Fox between-periods analysts and Nashville
Predators logos and time-outs with 45 seconds to play in a close game,
for all the Keith Primeaus trying to stickhandle, there is at least one
thing that has gotten better about the game, one thing that has enabled
us to remove the gun barrels from our mouths, if only for a few weeks
every year or two. And that is the growth of the international game.

Now, finally, hockey has what few other sports can claim: a hotly contested parallel competition that exists apart from, yet complements and ultimately enriches, standard league play, one that fills players and fans with passion and patriotism. And, perhaps best of all, international tournaments provide North American hockey fans with something they never otherwise get: a meaningful competition with a strong dramatic arc and a swift, decisive resolution. No year-long struggles for the eighth playoff spot, no three-month post-season marathon dances that drag wearily to a climax few people care to witness. In international play it all boils down to one game: flags wave, fans sing, goals are met with wild, orgiastic celebration, anthems play, tears of joy are shed, and then, home the next day in city squares or civic centres, throngs pour love on their heroes. It's the next best thing to your hometown team winning the Stanley Cup, and there are those who say it's even better.

For hockey fans in North America, it all began with the Summit Series in 1972, when only two countries, Canada and the Soviet Union, could claim to be the best in the world. Very gradually in the years and tournaments that followed, other countries arose to challenge the supremacy of those two, all leading up to the 1998 Olympics at Nagano, which ought to be remembered as a watershed moment in the international game. For Nagano—despite all the *Sturm und Drang* of four Canada Cups and its successor tournament, the World Cup—was the first authentic world championship of hockey ever played. There was a lot of grumbling about Nagano before and after the tournament— before, because it would somehow wreck the flow of the sacrosanct NHL regular season; after, because it showed just how far Canada had supposedly fallen as a hockey power, and the depth of boorish depravity the American players had supposedly plumbed in their Olympic Village rooms. But we could not disagree more.

At Nagano, for the first time ever, there would be full professional participation, all the best players in the world representing their nations in a wintertime tournament, as opposed to the summertime Canada Cups and World Cups that had borne the international hockey standard in the past. Because this was the Olympics, it meant that players would not sit the tournament out, as so many had the Canada Cup and World Cup. And, because this was the Olympics, it would have the attention of an international audience—not just Canadians, not just viewers of Channel 51 or something in the United States, but the full attention of U.S. network television and the American press, as well as the press of the world at large, something those other cup competitions had never gotten. Perhaps most important of all, the whole thing would be played on neutral ice, not conferring automatic home-ice advantage upon one nation or another—which is to say, Canada, whose claim to world hockey supremacy for the past two decades is based entirely on having played all its top-flight international games at home.

For the first time as well, players from Europe had reached the same level as North American players. Gone were the days when Tapio Levo and Jiri Bubla were the best some countries could produce. So many could now boast a superstar or two as good if not better than the best players from these shores—the Russians, Fedorov and Bure; the Swedes, Forsberg and Sundin; the Czechs, Jagr and Hasek; the Finns, Selanne and Koivu; Bondra for the Slovaks—any of them a match for Gretzky,

Sakic, Lindros, Yzerman, Roy, or certainly Keith Primeau, Adam Foote, Rob Zamuner, or anyone else Canada had to offer. Or the best of the Americans, who had shocked Canada in the 1996 World Cup: Brett Hull, Keith Tkachuk, Pat LaFontaine, Jeremy Roenick, Chris Chelios, Mike Richter, John LeClair, and more.

And indeed, the Olympic tournament at Nagano provided many exciting moments along the way—Canada beating the U.S., 4-1, and gaining a measure of revenge for the '96 World Cup defeat; unheralded Belarus and Kazakhstan, two former Soviet republics, surprising everyone by edging Slovakia and Germany to advance from the preliminary round; Pavel Bure's astonishing five-goal performance for Russia against the Finns in the semifinal. After single-handedly dismissing the Americans by stopping 38 of 39 shots in the U.S.-Czech quarterfinal, Dominik Hasek produced one of the all-time great moments in hockey history, although we'll bet our bottom dollar that 25 years later the CBC won't be airing any weepy retrospectives about it. Hasek and the Czechs shut down Canada's best, time and again, through 59 minutes of suspense-drenched semifinal action (it wasn't all Hasek in this game; the Czechs simply smothered Team Canada with a near-perfect neutral-zone trap). Finally, in the desperate closing moments, Canada's Trevor Linden scored to force overtime, and if you listened closely you could hear the thundering hooves of TV producers across Toronto stampeding to their tape libraries in search of slow-motion footage of prairie children mouthing the words to the national anthem, stalwart Inuit standing in the cold northern fastness, and all the other standard "I Can Hear Canada Singing" imagery. But no, Hasek lifted his game even higher in sudden death, and finally, unbreachable, stared down five straight Canadian shooters—Fleury, Bourque, Nieuwendyk, Lindros, and Shanahan—to seal the Czech triumph and tame those rampaging producers.

Best of all, the Olympic tournament played out as a classic storybook tale, reaching its climax with the perfect finish: success at last for the Czech Republic, a little country that had never won anything at the pinnacle of world play, save for one IIHF world championship in 1996 and three as Czechoslovakia in the 1970s, each of them watered down because most of the best NHL players were still tied up in the Stanley Cup playoffs. To make the Czechs' Olympic triumph all the sweeter, their victory in the gold-medal game came against their old nemesis, Russia, successor to the hated Soviet Union whose tanks had snuffed out the Prague Spring of 1968 and occupied their country for the next two decades. What better script could one ask for? The underdog—a country desperately in need of a symbolic triumph, having lost Slovakia in a peaceful but dispiriting 1993 divorce and still enduring a widespread economic and political malaise—snatching unexpected, unprecedented victory. This Olympic tournament provided us the unforgettable sight of 100,000 people jamming Prague's Old Town Square in the predawn hours to watch the gold-medal game on jerry-rigged video screens, and then the explosion of joy when the Czechs won the gold medal. The next day, the square filled again for the celebration, and the jubilant players showered the crowd with champagne and love, exulting together in their triumph at the biggest party the nation had seen since the Velvet Revolution threw off Communist rule without bloodshed nine years before. It was a marvelous upset, the little guy prevailing against all odds. Isn't that the classic sports story? Isn't that all we can ask from any sports event?

Yet all you heard about the Olympic hockey tournament, thanks to the NHL's woeful mishandling of what should have been a public-relations triumph, was what a fiasco it was. Why? Because Canada and the United States failed to bring home medals; because the American players broke a few chairs in their Olympic Village rooms (32 mentions in *The New York Times* between February 20 and April 20!); because it diverted attention from the "real business" of the NHL regular season; because the three-week Olympic break "disrupted" the NHL schedule, forcing teams to take a three-games-in-four-nights road trip six times instead of five during the league's already grossly overextended slate.

That's all rubbish. The Olympic tournament was great—great to see hockey played intensely, yet cleanly, free of the mindless violence that's always a threat to break out in any game in North America. And it was great, not because Canada, the United States, or the Russians could win—and not because they didn't—but because the Czech Republic, Sweden, Finland, and many other countries could also play competitively at the highest international level and have a chance to win it all.

There is nothing in sports like a closely contested world championship tournament between teams from different nations. Most North Americans are not really familiar with this phenomenon, because the sports we tend to care about here don't really exist on a world level. Football is utterly bereft of any international dimension, unless you count the exhibition games the old American Football League occasionally played against CFL teams. And you certainly don't want to count any-thing involving the Rhein Fire as "international," unless the sight of lapsed Crips from South Central butting heads with steroid-bloated Nebraska farmboys before a dimly appreciative crowd of Catalan-speak-ing tram drivers strikes you as an international sports event. Then there's baseball, which ought to be an international sport by now, what with so many Dominicans and Puerto Ricans and the occasional Cuban, Canadian, Japanese, Mexican, Venezuelan, Korean, and Australian populating major league line-ups (players from 17 countries other than the United States made up about one-third of big-league ros-ters in 1998). Two professional leagues have flourished for years in Japan. But despite this, baseball is not a world sport: perhaps it's still a hangover from the Reagan era, when baseball wrapped itself in a dull, inward-looking cloak of nostalgia and stars-and-stripes jingosim, but the prospect of seeing a true U.S national team play a true Dominican or Japanese national team seems about as distant as ever.

And then there's basketball, which has broad appeal all over the world—second only to soccer, albeit a distant second, but second nev-ertheless. There are strong domestic basketball leagues in Europe and thriving, viable ones in Asia and South America, and women's pro leagues are flourishing in various countries around the world as well. Some of the best players in the National Basketball Association come from places like Nigeria, Lithuania, Yugoslavia, Croatia, Germany, and the English- and Spanish-speaking Caribbean. Yet despite this diversity and the worldwide interest that NBA stars now command, the United States stands so far above the rest that there is simply no competition, no mystery, no drama in the fledgling international tournaments that pro basketball has lately begun to traffic in. The travesty of the U.S. Dream Team experience at the 1992 and 1996 Olympics was deeply sickening on so many levels: the sight of Michael Jordan and Scottie Pippen deliberately humiliating their future Chicago Bulls teammate Toni Kukoc to make some kind of point about contract money; of Charles Barkley elbowing Angolans under the basket as if to assert some kind of world-straddling, or in his case earth-girdling, greatness; of the rest of the Americans laughing and giggling and guffawing as they ran up the score on little third-rate basketball countries, all while the nauseating scene was fawningly narrated by American network announcers—all this was stomach-turning. But worse than that—*worse than that*—was how the poor schmucks who were beaten by 75 and 100 points bought into it all, begging their condescending tormentors for high-fives, autographs, and group photos. It made us wish the Dream Team had been playing, say, Albania, with Tie Domi starting at point guard.

Perhaps North America's inexperience in international team sports helps explain why our response to a quarter century of international hockey has been so naive. The sports that are truly global in scope— soccer, rugby, and cricket—are little followed on these shores, especially the latter two. But whereas in men's basketball the United States will win every time and until very recently in hockey it was either Canada or the old Soviet Union on top, in rugby there has long been a highly competitive international environment. World titles have routinely circulated among New Zealand, England, France, Wales, South Africa,

Australia, Scotland, and Ireland, with Argentina, Italy, and Pacific nations like Samoa, Tonga, and Fiji always fielding legitimate sides as well. In rugby there is usually a real mystery about who will win any given world tournament, and that makes for a fascinating competition rather than a march to a coronation. Cricket, too, offers up mystery and real competition, no matter how stupid you might think the game actually is. The field of contenders is wholly limited to old British Empire outposts, but within these confines it's still anybody's game: India, England, Pakistan, Australia, Sri Lanka, New Zealand, or the united West Indies, which is itself made up of strong constituent elements from Trinidad and Tobago, Jamaica, Barbados, Guyana, and other wind-caressed Caribbean points where they know how to reverse sweep a bodyline googly to silly mid-off with the best of 'em.

Soccer, of course, needs no introduction; it is the king of sports, played everywhere in the world. No fewer than 37 different nations have won at least one continental championship, and seven have won the World Cup, the largest, most passionately followed sporting event on the planet. The emotion generated by an international soccer match, inside the stadium and out, beggars description. It is literally true that wars always stop for a big game, and that on one occasion a war began because of one, that an oppressed people can find their only means of free expression through their support of a certain team, that dictators have manipulated games to keep their citizens in line, that a certain outcome can topple governments, that whole countries erupt in joy or in tears, that people are driven to murder or suicide or pour dancing into boulevards by the hundreds of thousands, all because of the Beautiful Game. We know, because we've been there when it has happened, and it's the most emotionally overwhelming mass hysteria you could possibly imagine. It's magic, fantastic, better than any drug.

Now hockey has entered this worldly realm of intoxicating passion, even if it is difficult to imagine that kind of passion being generated by the likes of Adam Deadmarsh. But in any case, the lesson of English soccer may be instructive to the various parliamentary committees now grappling with Canada's new, more humble station in the hockey world.

After creating the rules of soccer in the latter half of the 19th century and spreading the game throughout the world in the early years of the 20th, haughty England withdrew in silent majesty from most international competition. Paul Gardner, in his history of soccer, *The Simple Game*, notes that England had amassed a 24-1-1 record against foreign opponents, all in meaningless exhibitions, before meeting the class of the continent, Austria, in London in 1932. "England won the game 4-3, but there were many who thought the better team had lost. The English, having gained the expected result, paid no attention to the inventiveness of the Austrians' soccer ... and so the English went on believing they had nothing to learn." In 1950, England travelled to Brazil to enter its first World Cup tournament, and promptly lost 1-0 to the lowly United States in what is still considered the greatest upset in soccer history. Within a couple of years England had lost at home for the first time ever, and ever since, the homeland of soccer, despite always fielding excellent teams, has consistently disappointed on the international stage. Well, almost always: the only time it won the World Cup was in 1966, when, tellingly, the tournament was held in England.

Does any of this sound familiar to Canadian hockey fans? The automatic assumption, based on being the country that founded the game, of innate superiority? The narrow victory, by 4-3 yet, over a creative foreign opponent? The longstanding reluctance to play anywhere but at home? And the shocking defeat, many years later, in a long-overdue trip overseas?

Is the current Canadian perception that Canada has fallen from the lofty heights of hockey supremacy an entirely accurate one? Or is it false, fuelled by a lack of global perspective and by ignorance of what European hockey is and where it comes from? Are all the 25-part newspaper series decrying the sudden erosion in stickhandling skills among the children of the True North Strong and Free and, concomitantly, the rise of humane coaching techniques in Scandinavia, truly on the mark? Is it really the way Canadian hockey pundits tell us it is in the aftermath of the 1998 Olympics, with the towering blond Godzilla of Nordic hockey wading through our cities, smashing our antiquated ideas with enlightened tracts on practising backward crossovers, while just offshore the giant flying rocket turtle of the Eastern European game demonstrates just how weak our puny weapons are?

We would argue no, there are *no flying rocket turtles*. But more to the point, we would argue first that Canada may never have stood alone atop the hockey world. That's right, never. Before 1972, the notion that

Canada was the undisputed king of the hill was never actually put to the
test. There was simply no interaction between Canada's best and anybody else's best. Certainly in '72, when the Soviets dumbfounded Team
Canada in the Summit Series, it was clear enough right there and then
that the Soviets at least were the Canadians' equal. After that harrow-
ing experience, Team Canada never again travelled off this continent to
play anybody, until it went to Nagano in '98. Incredible as it may seem,
Canada's assumption that it was No. 1 was based on the fact that it
always played at home.

Canada's ruinous underestimation of European hockey, like
England's ruinous underestimation of soccer beyond the Channel, has
always been informed by a certain amount of ignorance. The most
fundamental gap in our knowledge seems to be in the origins of
hockey as it was played in Scandinavia and Russia. Almost always,
when you read histories of Russian hockey written in North
America, there is some passing mention of bandy or some other
unexplained hockeylike Ur-game played there before the Russians
adopted six-man Canadian hockey in the late 1940s. This wildly
incomplete version of history has reinforced the impression that the
game sprang up in Europe out of whole cloth, especially in the
Soviet Union, and that the Soviets got so good so fast because their
totalitarian government poured the weight of its resources into the
development of Canadian-style hockey there. Then waddaya know,
just eight years later in 1956, the U.S.S.R. wins its first Olympic gold
medal and has suddenly become the dominant force in international
hockey. But this version of history misconstrues or just plain leaves

out much of what is important to know about European hockey and the way it is played.

That "innocuous ball-and-stick game" that's always glossed over so glibly—bandy—has a long tradition in Russia and Scandinavia, one that recalls hockey's roots in Canada in the 19th and early 20th centuries. And bandy is still around today; if you have a good search engine on your computer, you can browse the Internet and find sites devoted to bandy, or as the Russians themselves refer to it, "Russian hockey." It'll be a real revelation for you, as it was for us.

Bandy is played outdoors, on a sheet of ice the size of a soccer field surrounded by six-inch-high boards, with 11 men a side; players wear skates and use field-hockey-like sticks to propel a ball rather than a puck. The players all wear helmets, shinpads, and gloves very much like hockey gear; the goalies wear hockey-style goalie pads but do not have sticks or large catching gloves. The nets are about 7 feet high and 11 1/2 feet wide, roughly splitting the difference between hockey and soccer nets. The most crucial difference between bandy and hockey is that in bandy there is no checking; the body-contact rules are most similar to those in soccer. The game is usually played in front of a few hundred to perhaps two or three thousand spectators, because *it's freezing out there*, but despite these relatively sparse crowds, it has been played as a spectator sport for more than 100 years. Because of the nature of the rules of bandy, a premium is placed on passing and skating, and—where it differs most from the development of Canadian hockey—the ability to attack and defend without hitting.

"Soviet histories of hockey make passing reference to versions of bandy played in numerous locations in the last decades of the 19th century," writes Robert Edelman in his superb book *Serious Fun: A History of Spectator Sports in the USSR*.

> By 1901, regularly scheduled games were taking place in the capital
> [Petersburg] among teams representing many of the same clubs that
> had fielded soccer teams. By 1905, organized hockey had spread to
> Moscow and Tver, and by 1910, clubs and city select teams were jour-
> neying to meet opponents in other towns. These games could attract
> as many as one or two thousand spectators willing to brave the cold.

This sounds remarkably similar to what we all know of six- and seven-man hockey's earliest days in Canada—small crowds watching a developing game at outdoor rinks in the middle of a cold country's winter.

The Russian Revolution and the civil war that followed disrupted Russian hockey, as it did all sports in Russia, until the mid-1920s. Between 1923 and 1936, there were city championships and an irregular national tournament. In 1936, organization improved, leading to league play and a cup competition. "The same sports societies that dominated soccer fielded the leading hockey teams," writes Edelman. "Dinamo, Spartak, Central Army, Metallurg, Krylia Sovietov, and Lokomotiv were just a few of the stronger clubs, all of which supported women's teams as well. On the rare days with good weather, as many as 30,000 might attend a game between top teams at Moscow's Dinamo Stadium or at Lenin Stadium in Leningrad."

Meanwhile, the Soviets were very much aware of Canadian hockey, which had become popular in the 1920s and 1930s in western and central Europe. In sports newspapers, writers and athletes would occasionally speculate on how the Soviets would do if they tried the Canadian version of the game. But World War II intervened, to put it mildly, and no real attempt was made to stage a match recognizable as the hockey we know until the war ended.

The signal moment for the modern, western style of the game in the Soviet Union occurred on February 17, 1946, when a crowd of several thousand attending a bandy match, played at the Moscow Institute of Physical Culture, stuck around as primitive boards were set up and witnessed the first exhibition of Canadian-style hockey. The game was a big success, and that fall a league was formed in which the top clubs competed. This is the point at which North American histories of Canadian-style hockey in the Soviet Union usually begin. But although the game might be said to have been born there in 1946, it was only after having been conceived in the 19th century and undergoing a long gestation through the first half of the 20th.

> Western journalistic descriptions of the Soviet hockey program,
> [Edelman points out] have usually ignored the enormous importance
> of Russian hockey. The Soviets did not start from scratch, as many
> accounts have suggested. Such claims ascribe subsequent Soviet suc-
> cess in hockey to the power of the sports system, with its scientific
> methods amid lavish state support, fueled by ideologically generated
> political fanaticism. By ignoring the prehistory of hockey, one can be
> easily led to that far-from-correct conclusion.... In fact, Soviet hockey
> players simply adapted to a different version of a game that was fun-
> damentally similar to the Russian hockey they had played for decades.

Not only was body contact foreign to Russian hockey, the Soviets, when they switched to Canadian hockey, made a deliberate effort to keep it clean. In 1949, referee Sergei Savin told *Sovietskii Sport*: "Hockey in our country develops by its own path and has nothing in common with foreign versions of the game. There, players follow the worst example of Canadian professional hockey, try always to fight, and replace technique with crude physical force." This perfect summation of the Russian philosophy towards the game remained in force well into the 1980s. North Americans never understood that this was a central tenet for the so-called Big Red Machine.

The Russian strategy and style that would so baffle various Team Canadas down through the years, as Edelman perfectly describes, "eschewed the Canadians' characteristic use of individual stickhandling, checking, grabbing and long-distance shooting for an attacking style that placed primary attention on the men without the puck, whose job, like a soccer player's, was to find empty space in order to receive penetrating passes."

Anatoli Tarasov was the coach who would shape the entire Soviet hockey program, and Vsevolod Bobrov, already a world-class athlete in soccer and a top player in Russian hockey, would become the brightest star in Tarasov's system. With Tarasov behind the bench and Bobrov leading the way, the Soviet national team made its first appearance in the European and World Championships in 1954 and won them both. Two years later, they made their debut in the Olympics and again came away with the gold.

Soviet supremacy in Olympic competition, starting in the 1950s, soon became a sore point in the West, which consoled itself by repeat-ing ad nauseam that the Soviets were full-time hockey players, amateurs in name only, and that their "professionals" couldn't even lace up our professionals' skates. The NHL arranged the eight-game Summit Series in '72 to prove the point, and however much the Soviet authorities sought to use the clash for their own propaganda purposes, the jingois-tic drum-beating on this side of the Atlantic was deafening.

Every hockey pundit in North America sneered that the team of NHL all-stars would win all eight games by blow-out scores, that any result less than that would be a phenomenal upset and a national dis-grace, and the players, sounding a little traumatized by the hype and the expectations put on them, agreed. For a few minutes it all went accord-ing to script, as the mighty NHL stars encountered no resistance in jumping out to a swift 2-0 lead in Game 1 in the hallowed Montreal Forum amid the laughter of the Canadians; as Vladislav Tretiak remem-bers in his grandly titled memoir, Tretiak, the Legend, "Phil Esposito, who scored the [first] goal, patronizingly tapped me on my shoulder," and, "when Henderson scored their second goal, after just six minutes, the crowd flew into a triumphant rage. The organist played a funeral march."

Then everything went flooey. The Soviets put into play their swirling rushes and refused to respond to the heavy checking of the Canadians. Within 11 minutes they had tied it up, and at the end of two periods, they led by 2. The Soviets won going away, 7-3, leaving the NHLers to stumble off glassy-eyed at game's end. Team Canada won just once in the four games on Canadian ice, and by the time the series was set to resume in the Soviet Union, the NHL, assisted by the North American hockey press, had manufactured more excuses than goals. The Russians are "robots"—*they won't swing their fists when we hack and abuse them!* They're more motivated—*they'll be sent to Siberia if they lose!* They play together all year, and we've only been together a few weeks! They're vicious with their sticks—*they don't care if they cut your throat or put your eye out!* The whole tournament was fitted with a Cold War political yoke—our wholesome way of life against *their godless communist system.* Turmoil racked the team as players who went unused chafed in frustration, were pressured to return home by their NHL clubs, and were vilified as unpatriotic troublemakers by Team Canada management, who in turn whined about how hard it was to win on the road and how terrible the Moscow hotels and food were.

The NHLers gooned it up throughout the series, most infamously when a wicked two-handed slash by Bobby Clarke—acting on orders from John Ferguson, the former Canadiens cement-head who, astoundingly, had been made an assistant coach—broke the ankle of the stylish Soviet star Valeri Kharlamov. In the seventh game, Esposito threatened Soviet captain Boris Mikhailov by drawing his finger across his throat in a cold-blooded pantomime (later on, Gary Bergman did it too), the same gesture that, when made by NBA players a generation later, would horrify observers as something out of a ghetto crack war. In the eighth and deciding game, the Canadians let it all hang out, going full-goose-bonzo ballistic. In a lunatic atmosphere that seemed part riot, part demolition derby, part gladiatorial combat, Bergman took a swing at the penalty-box timekeeper; Bill White deliberately fired the puck at the referee; J.P. Parise swooped in during a stoppage, stick raised, and menaced the referee with imminent decapitation; coach Harry Sinden threw a sustained tantrum, flinging chairs onto the ice; and stick-brandishing Canadian players went nose-to-nose with Soviet police who attempted to restrain team organizer and future felon Alan Eagleson when a raging Eagleson vaulted several rows of seats to challenge the goal judge.

What was as amazing as anything during this circus of insanity was the Canadian commentators' ability to look at the behaviour of the Canadian players, coaches, and team management, and somehow manage to construe the Soviets' understandable reaction to it all—shock, mainly—as psychologically aberrant. Canadians had done what most people do during a war: dehumanize the enemy to make it easy to hate them and do things to hurt them. The Soviets, remember, were robots—and we would insist on calling them that for some 20 years, a strange trope, given all the times we saw them embracing and whooping it up on the ice, celebrating goals, gold medals, and championships.

In the end, the NHL took the Flyer route through the Soviet Union, hacking and clubbing the Soviet players like seal pups and bullying their way to a thrilling, remarkable comeback. The NHL stars carved out three tense, close wins, the last on Paul Henderson's goal with a minute to go in the final game. The 4-3-1 series margin was immediately proclaimed the greatest triumph in the history of sport, and maybe it was. But for all the cheering it set off, Canada, in the back of its collective mind, knew that something greater had been lost. More than a quarter century later that series is still endlessly revisited, probed and debated and examined in minute detail in a search for meaning and what it says about the Canadian national identity, a problematic landmark in the national consciousness. The team's narrow victory on the scoreboard masked a larger and more important defeat—that of Canada's image as an unassailable hockey superpower—and that it had been nearly bested by what it had regarded as a third-rate opponent was a shock to the system. Henderson's goal and the celebrations it touched off obscured the real point: the cloistered, self-absorbed North American version of the game, in smugly assuming its way was the only way, had stagnated.

Indeed Canada's victory may have done more harm to North American hockey than good. By winning, the Canadian hockey establishment was able to put off what many fans already saw to be true: that the European game was different, and that it was every bit as good as, maybe even better than, the Canadian one. Worse, that Team Canada won through brutality, poor sportsmanship, and, let's face it, cheating (even today, the fact that the Czechoslovakian referees actually called elbowing and tripping when the Canadians elbowed and tripped players is remembered as terrible, even corrupt officiating), was magically reinterpreted as winning through stronger will. Imagine the reaction had it been Soviets who hacked and clubbed Canadians, who made throat-slitting gestures, who broke the ankles of Canadian wingers, who vaulted out of the stands to wrestle with Canadian cops.

But we are not here to besmirch the boys of '72, we're just here to do a little revisionist history. The NHLers were playing the rugged North American form of the game, and the Soviets were playing theirs, the one that sprang from the huge ice fields and no-body-contact ethos of bandy—and it served them well. In 1974, the Soviets dismantled the WHA version of Team Canada, the one with Hull and Howe on it. In 1975-76, two of the USSR's club teams, the Wings of the Soviet and CSKA (that's Central Sports Club of the Army, the team North Americans always referred to as Red Army, even though the word "Red" was never part of the club's name), augmented by a handful of players from other Soviet elite league teams, came over and outskated, out-skilled, and outwitted most of the best NHL teams. The only game Central Army lost was when the Flyers disgraced not just themselves but all of North American hockey with an exhibition of malevolent brutality unprecedented by even the Flyers' own notorious standards of troglodyte mayhem.

That game, pitting the Stanley Cup holders against the champions of the Soviet elite league, was, in effect, for the club championship of the world. Any excuse that the Canadians had proffered for earlier hiccups in '72 and '74—our players were unused to playing together, we didn't have enough time to jell as a team, we weren't playing in the middle of the hockey season, the Soviets were an unknown quantity we weren't prepared for, the Moscow hotels were bad, it's impossible to get vinegar with your french fries anywhere in this goddamn worker's paradise because there are KGB men everywhere (there probably were)—would not apply here. The game would be played on January 11, in Philadelphia, broadcast on national television in both the United States and Canada, and the army team was full of players everyone was now familiar with. We looked forward to it as much as we'd looked forward to Game 8 of the Summit Series.

Every hockey fan remembers where he or she was when Henderson scored that goal with a minute to go in '72, and so do we. But we remember just as vividly the first 11 minutes of that CSKA-Flyers game. It was the single most disgraceful episode ever perpetrated in the history of a sport chockful of disgraceful episodes; the Eddie Shore-Ace Bailey incident, the Richard Riot and the events leading up to it, Dale Hunter deliberately injuring Pierre Turgeon while Turgeon celebrated a series-clinching goal, anything Billy Smith or Ron Hextall ever did with their sticks, you name it, nothing was ever as cynical or ugly as what the Flyers did that day. From the opening draw, the Flyers hacked, slashed, elbowed, blindsided, kneed, crosschecked, kicked, pummelled, and cheapshotted the army team with demonic glee and without hindrance from the Canadian officiating crew. The Soviets, as was their custom, stoically turned the other cheek time and again, waiting for referee Lloyd Gilmour to call a penalty. But despite 10 minutes of this one-sided savagery, Gilmour found his whistle only often enough to give the Soviets two power plays to the Flyers' one. Seconds after defenceman Ed Van Impe returned to the ice from the penalty box, he zeroed in on Kharlamov, decking the Russian and pounding him insensate. At that point, CSKA coach Konstantin Loktev made the unprecedented but entirely understandable move of pulling his team off the ice, vowing not to return without some assurance for his players' safety. Eagleson countered by threatening to withhold any money owed the Soviet hockey federation for their participation in the series. After 18 minutes, CSKA reappeared on the ice, but basically just went through the motions, getting outshot 49-13 and losing 4-1, although they at least emerged with their lives. It was shameful, appalling. We wished some gaping hell-mouth would open in the ice and suck the Flyers down to whatever sulphurous pit had spawned them. Eternal disgrace to the Philadelphia Flyers, their management, and yes, to their fans, all of whom still celebrate this game as a highlight in that franchise's ugly, ugly history.

The North American sports press was almost unanimous in fawning over this hideous exhibition, winking at the atrocity and gloating over the courageous win, once again attributing it to the NHLers' superior will. *The Hockey News* game report called the Flyer victory "almost perfect," noting that "Shero's Flyers rose to the occasion with a super checking job…. The Flyers did play rough, but not nearly as rough as in many NHL games. Andre Dupont put the blade of his stick on Mikhailov's nose and suggested he might get worse in a later confrontation. 'After that he was very nice to me. He never came near me,' grinned Dupont later."

Meanwhile, *Hockey News* editor and publisher Ken McKenzie found new reasons to suspect Soviet treachery: "Philadelphia Flyers showed the hockey public that the Stanley Cup champions are truly the best in the world. Overcoming Soviet ploys to throw them off their game, such as showing up late for luncheons, complaining about gifts and even storming off the ice in their crucial match, the Flyers have to be commended for their supreme effort." Those sinister Rooskies.

Reality obtruded in *The Hockey News* a week later, however, in the form of a letter from a fan in New Jersey.

Watching the Russian-NHL series was certainly educational to me, [he wrote.] It proved beyond a doubt that not only are the Russians better hockey players, they show much more class. Apparently embarrassed by being outplayed by the Russians, the NHL teams resorted to ignorant violence to retaliate. Time after time, the NHL punched, charged and crosschecked the Russians unnecessarily, obviously trying to prove their manhood. The coup de grace was Wayne Cashman's slash [in the CSKA-Boston game]. He could have killed or maimed the Russian he hit very easily. Then, Phil Esposito showed his intelligence in an interview several minutes later by saying he was glad Cashman did it. Then the announcer insinuated the Russian was faking being injured.... I am not a Russian or a Communist. I am a Vietnam veteran and proud to be an American. But I am giving up being a hockey fan, and going back to baseball.

Tretiak, CSKA's goaltender, recalls the January 11 game in his memoir: "We didn't know before that a pack of barbarians could put on skates and get away with hunting hockey players in front of thousands of spectators."

The Flyers' victory at the end of that 1975-76 tour sealed Canada's personality in international play: nasty, brutish, and short-tempered. Nevertheless, for the NHL, though it would never admit it at the time, these first close looks at EuroSoviet hockey were a revelation. The Soviets had confounded the Canadians with their swirling, cycling, criss-crossing patterns of attack and emphasis on skating and passing, the very antithesis of the straight-up-and-down, lane-bound North American style in which hitting and shooting were supreme. But slowly the North Americans started to absorb some of that style.

It started with the Swedes Borje Salming and Inge Hammarstrom, who came over to play for Toronto and became the objects of excited curiosity, like the first Indians shipped back to Tudor England for exhibition. The assertion made by vulgarian Toronto owner Harold Ballard—that a Swedish player "could go into the corner with six eggs in his pocket and not break any of them"—absurdly tarred Scandinavian players for years as delicate, unmanly, easily intimidated players, "Chicken Swedes," despite the fact that Salming soon established himself as one of the most courageous, as well as one of the most skilful, defencemen in hockey.

Meanwhile, the WHA, motivated as much by a desperate need for players as by any transcendent faith in the worthiness of Europeans, took to recruiting Swedes, Finns, and Czechoslovakians and discovered their skills were all they'd hoped for and more. Winnipeg won the Avco World Trophy (this may be the last time you ever see those three words together in print) with several Europeans on their roster, most famously Ulf Nilsson and Anders Hedberg, who were teamed with Hull. By the end of the 1970s it was rare to find a team in either league without one or two Europeans in the line-up, either imports from Sweden and Finland or defectors from Czechoslovakia. The drawback was that while North American teams, with or without EuroSoviet players, were soon busily trying to incorporate the EuroSoviet style of attack, the art of defence had badly deteriorated through the talent-thinning expansions of the 1970s and the influence of Flyer-inspired clutch-and-grab tactics. Forwards, no longer hindered by the old up-and-down-the-wing patterns, now described free-form arcs around baffled, stationary defenders and fired away at will. As the '70s turned into the '80s, 4-3 scores turned into 6-5 and 9-7; scoring mushroomed as the Age of Air Hockey flourished.

By now, the Americans had started getting good. The 1980 Olympic team, the product of a U.S. hockey boom in the 1960s and '70s, won the gold medal. By the end of the '80s, every team had at least three or four Americans on the roster; 10 years earlier it had been remarkable for any team to have more than one. Team Canada limped through the decade, playing at home throughout, getting slaughtered by the Soviets in the '81 Canada Cup final 8-1, sweeping Sweden in a relatively easy two-game Canada Cup final in 1984, but only after squeaking past the U.S.S.R. in overtime in the semifinal, and needing last-second heroics to beat the Soviets two out of three in 1987. That last result left Team Canada, as well as various NHL club and all-star teams, with a 23-39-5 record against Soviet club and national teams, even though 63 of those 67 games had been played on Canadian or American ice.

In '91 Team Canada had little trouble sweeping the Americans in the Canada Cup final, but by the middle of the decade there were as many American stars as Canadian; all the Americans lacked was someone of the stature of Gretzky or Lemieux. Meanwhile, big North American dollars and rampant expansion brought more and more Europeans into the NHL. European leagues became mere husks of their former selves, little more than AHLs and OHLs with umlauts. The clincher was the influx into the NHL of Soviet players, starting in the late '80s with the defection of Alexander Mogilny and the player rebellion, led by Vyacheslav Fetisov, against the Soviet hockey federation. In the early

'90s, the Soviet Union collapsed outright and players started coming over in droves, while the old Soviet elite league withered into something resembling a garage league.

By the mid '90s, the number of Europeans and Americans on NHL rosters had skyrocketed, accounting for almost 50 percent of the league's players. The NHL's most marketable player was a Russian, Sergei Fedorov; its best goalie a Czech, Dominik Hasek; its most creative defenceman an American, Brian Leetch, and its best and most exciting player, Mario Lemieux, a Canadian, was about to retire because he couldn't stand the game anymore. Finally, in 1996, the U.S. national team took an aging Team Canada twice in a row in Hamilton, to claim the World Cup.

Which brings us to 1998, and an awful lot of northern hand-wringing. The Czech Republic wins the Olympic gold medal. Seven of the top 11 scorers in the NHL are Europeans. Players like Hasek, Jagr, Selanne (the three finalists for the 1998 Hart Trophy, the first time ever that Europeans swept the honour), Fedorov, Forsberg, and Sundin eclipse Canadian-born talent as the league's crème de la crème. Canada's junior team finishes seventh at the world junior championships, and the Canadian women's team is unseated as world champions by the Americans at Nagano. Canadians are distraught, which at least is a healthy sign, because they want to be on top again, just as Brazil or Italy do when they erupt in national wailing and vegetable-throwing following a reverse in soccer.

But the problem, as we have seen in looking back at Canada's record from the Summit Series on, is that Canada may never really have been on top in hockey. Canadians think their hockey insularity ended in 1972, and to a certain extent that is true; North America started to import European players and absorbed European tactics and strategies, and it certainly stepped up its participation in international play, but only to a limited degree. After Henderson's goal in Moscow, Canada never again put itself to a true test. Like England in soccer before World War II, Canada merely dabbled in international play under carefully controlled conditions, getting narrow results that only seemed to confirm its primacy. When it finally strode onto the world stage in earnest in 1998, as England did in 1950, it received a rude shock. The rest of the world had caught up—or, more accurately, it found out that the rest of the world had caught up a long time ago.

But look here: what's wrong with being one of six or seven nations that can claim to be the world's best? Isn't it more interesting than being the only big fish in a small pond? Us, we'll take being a fairly large fish, battling it out with a few other fishes of comparable size, in a pond that's a little bigger than it used to be. With Nagano, hockey became the first North American professional team sport to join that select international fraternity of truly global sports. It would be a shame if the NHL were to retreat from these lofty heights just because of the whining of those unhappy with the Canadians' and Americans' disappointing finish, or of those deprived of two weeks' worth of San Jose-Phoenix games. We'll take the drama of Hasek versus Lindros over that every time.

And still, and yet... while Nagano had its share of glittering moments, there was something more disappointing, more disquieting, than any Canadian or American underachievement, and it is more important to hockey's big picture than those temporary national setbacks.

Think of the gold-medal game. High drama to be sure, but the game itself was, well, dull. It was tentative, cautious hockey, played at a walking pace. There were precious few real scoring chances, and any shot that did get through (only 20 by Russia, 21 by the Czechs) was smothered by amply padded goalies who hardly had to move to get in its way. Was this an Olympic gold-medal game between Russia and the Czech Republic, or was this a typical NHL regular-season game? In fact, when you think about the rest of the hockey games in these Olympics, they looked just as similarly dreary as any the NHL now specializes in. Even in the tense semifinal between the Czechs and Canada, outside of Linden's dramatic tying goal and Hasek's heroics in the shootout, play was for the most part, slow, constricted, full of obstruction, with a total of only 47 shots in regulation time. And so it went for too many games in the tournament—the same problems that plague the NHL now seem to plague international play. Consider the top 10 Olympic goalies in terms of save percentage:

Kolzig, Germany	.966
Hasek, Czech Republic	.961
Heiss, Germany	.955
Roy, Canada	.935
Shtalenkov, Russia	.931
Imoo, Japan	.925
Huet, France	.925
Gravel, France	.923
Sulander, Finland	.918
Shumidub, Belarus	.917

Aleksandr Shumidub of Belarus! .917! And he's only the 10th-best goalie in a 14-team tournament! *Dusty Imoo?! .925? Come on!* Do these numbers remind you of anything? If the evidence of your own eyes watching the games during the Olympics was not enough, then certainly these numbers should clinch the argument that, minus the fighting, international hockey now looks just the same as NHL hockey. And it should stand to reason, after all, since so many of Europe's best players play in the NHL, or the IHL, or the AHL, and the domestic leagues in Scandinavia and Russia are only shadows of what they once were.

In the past it was always a revelation to watch the teams from Europe who came to North America, precisely because they played the game so differently, because they even practised and warmed up differently (we attended the games of the Soviet team tours of the NHL in the '70s and '80s, and their pre-game sessions were so precisely organized and were executed at such a rapid pace that the drills alone looked intimidating). But now you see Russians and Czechs and Finns hanging around in the neutral zone, wrapping their arms around opposing forwards, getting their shots blocked as they fire without thought or design… it could be Russia we're watching, or it could be the Mighty Ducks of Anaheim. Who can tell? And really, it makes sense; no one outside of Don Cherry believes in "the chicken Swede" anymore. For well over a decade, rugged, heavy-hitting, even goonish Europeans have roamed North American rinks: Esa Tikkanen, Ulf Samuelsson, Tomas Sandstrom, Darius Kasparaitis, Vladimir Konstantinov before the unfortunate limousine accident, each of them as infuriating as any corn-fed western Canadian bruiser or nickel-mining Sudbury native;

even swift-skating superstars like Forsberg and Selanne take no guff from anyone.

Just as North Americans have absorbed much of what European hockey has to offer, so too have Europeans absorbed what North American hockey has to offer. Now, to the skating and passing and wide-open spaces born of their bandy roots, Europeans have added physicality, defence, caution, and enormous goalie equipment. The result: all over the world, hockey now looks the same.

When the game is dragged down to its lowest common denominator, when it becomes impossible to beat overpadded goalies, when you have to take 100 shots in order to get five goals (as you must, for that is the mathematical reality when you face a goalie with a .950 save percentage), any team is in a position to do well, to advance. In the NHL, the Florida Panthers and Washington Capitals can reach the Stanley Cup Final because John Vanbiesbrouck and Olaf Kolzig had such great years, and the often hilariously inept Buffalo Sabres can reach the semifinals simply because they have Dominik Hasek. And in international play, the same thing obtains, so that in the 1998 IIHF world championship, the United States, lacking stars but still carrying a roster full of NHLers, can lose to France, Italy, and Latvia, and Canada can get booted 7-1 by Sweden. And in the final, a two-game series between arch rivals Sweden and Finland? 1-0, and 0-0. Again, an eerie echo of the Olympic gold-medal game, of the Colorado Avalanche's 1997 Cup-clinching three-overtime 1-0 win, and of just about any old NHL or minor-league or junior-league game in any shopping mall of a rink on any dank, dreary November or February evening you care to name.

Not quite every team at Nagano looked like they had just popped out of the North American neutral-zone cookie-cutter. Watching Kazakhstan, none of whose players had ever skated in the NHL, was a weirdly nostalgic experience. There they were, this team clad in red, circling, swirling, arcing, at half the speed surely, but with the instincts, the purpose, the style of that earlier team that had taught North American hockey so many lessons about how the game could be played. And the Kazakhs did well, getting out of their preliminary group and staying competitive in their second-stage games, the last practitioners of the antique Soviet way. Strange that the style that had once seemed so radical, so new, so much the wave of the future could now look like such a throwback, but there they were, pleasing to watch, a living reminder of those distant times when a bunch of earnest Bolshevik athletes put down their short bandy sticks and picked up longer hockey sticks, when players in tattered uniforms stepped onto the ice at the Montreal Forum amid the condescending laughter of the Canadians and proceeded to turn the hockey world upside down.

As for the gnashing of teeth north of the longest undefended border on earth, we say go ahead and gnash. It's a good thing. Do many of the things all those 25-part newspaper series recommend: reform junior hockey so that teenagers aren't shuttled thousands of miles from home to play 80-game schedules that subject them to endless bus rides in the dead of winter and the predations, sexual and otherwise, of professional coaches on the make. Step away from the emphasis on size and organ-crushing body checks and fighting, and step closer to an emphasis on skills and creativity and joy in scoring beautiful goals. For god's sake don't build the rinks any wider than 200 feet by 85, because then the bad points of European hockey—a lax attitude towards defence and long, pointless intervals of perimeter play—will filter into the game here, but the very fact that even that is being considered is, we guess, a good sign, a sign Canadian hockey wants to break free from the bonds that have held it back, a sign it wants to reclaim its place as No. 1 in the world, even if it may never truly have held it in the first place. Here are two American boys who wouldn't mind at all if a reformed Canada started winning again. Go Canada go.

Secretly, though, we're still rooting for Kazakhstan.

Chapter 9

the game plan

"War is hell, but expansion is worse."
—Tom McVie, former coach of the Washington
Capitals, Winnipeg Jets and New Jersey Devils

The history of spectator sports in North America is littered with the
desiccated corpses of games that once were "hot," games that once drew
the fervid attention of big crowds and breathless press reports but
declined into obscurity and irrelevancy. Rowing was one of the most
popular spectator sports in turn-of-the-century North America, and in
the 1920s and '30s most big cities had velodromes that packed 'em in
for eight-day bicycle races. But the crowds eventually dwindled, and
now rowing and velodrome bike-racing register on the radar screen of
the sports world at large only once every four years, during the

Olympics. Other sports too have waned and faded down through the decades: prize fighting, thoroughbred racing, big-time track and field, all have slid from a place of central importance to the periphery, while lacrosse, pro wrestling, soccer, and beach volleyball oscillate through cycles of invisibility, fame, and invisibility again.

This is exactly what ought to frighten the men running the National Hockey League. For several generations, they've been certain of two things: that their game was No. 1 in Canada, and that it would move up from No. 4 in the United States. What they never thought of was this: that in Canada, the primacy of hockey could waver and crumble, in the same way that baseball is no longer king of the hill in the United States—and that in America, hockey could drop right out of the No. 4 position, that its place could be usurped by something new, hot, and on the way up.

Scary, unthinkable, impossible. Yet this is not a prospect to be dismissed or laughed off. This is exactly where hockey stands as the 1990s draw to a close. The NHL's television ratings in both countries are dropping like a stone, and even many of its loyal fans are tuning out. Practically no one, nonfans and fans alike, has anything good to say about the current state of the game. Gary Bettman can insist until he's blue in the face that hockey's doing just fine, but the fact remains that almost everyone disagrees. Meanwhile, the Women's National Basketball Association, in only its second year of existence, draws better U.S. television ratings than the NHL, with similar attendance averages and more positive media attention.

Even what should seem like a success for the NHL, the August 1998 signing of a new U.S. television contract with the Disney Corporation worth US$600 million, is widely seen as evidence of failure. Most press reports on the signing instead focused on the NHL's plunging ratings; the US$20 million annual losses suffered by the outgoing network, Fox, in carrying the league's games; the vote by 95 *percent* of Fox's local affiliates to stop carrying the NHL; Bettman's threat of a lawsuit if Fox didn't agree to honour the final year of its contract; the desperate quality of ABC and ESPN sports president Steve Bornstein's insistence that "we will make money on this deal." As media analyst Barry Hyman of the stock brokerage firm Ehrenkrantz King Nussbaum put it the day of the signing: "It's an exorbitant amount to pay. This is the NHL, not the NFL, not baseball."

Such today is the lowly standing of hockey, "the coolest game on earth," as columnists are mockingly calling it, appropriating the NHL's own suddenly off-key slogan. Hockey may not yet face the virtual extinction that front-page sports like rowing and indoor cycling quickly found, but on its current trajectory, a humble place in the demimonde of obscure cult sports is a very real danger. If the National Hockey League is to avoid this fate, if it is to win back its disaffected fans in Canada and the United States, if it is serious about trying to bring new fans to the game, if it wants to restore hockey's status as the most vibrant, electrifying sport in the world, it must take action now to protect and save the game.

Here's how to go about doing it.

The NHL's first order of business must be to call a moratorium on expansion, making the entrance of the Columbus Blue Jackets and the Minnesota, *ulp*, Wild for the 2000-01 season the final additions to the league. That would cap league membership at 30 clubs and put a halt to the unfettered growth that has proven so ruinous to the quality of play, schedule lengths, and fans' familiarity with teams and players. Owners would do well to remind themselves of a basic law of economics: when you create a supply that exceeds demand, the value of your product drops. By instituting a moratorium on expansion, the NHL would put an end to the oversupply that has diluted and cheapened the league.

Furthermore, an expansion halt would send a positive signal to disaffected fans, announcing to them that the men who run the NHL care about keeping the quality of play up to at least a certain level, that schedules stay in line, and that only those communities that truly want and deserve an NHL team get one, instead of just any old commuter sprawl with $80 million to spare.

That brings up another announcement that must be made to help restore fans' faith in the NHL: a declaration that the league is committed to do all it can to keep franchises in their current cities. The NHL must exhaust every possible remedy before allowing a club to move; in effect, the Board of Governors must agree that the only way they will allow a team to pull out of a city is if the fans of that city have not supported the team. The old California Seals, Kansas City Scouts, and Colorado Rockies, with their attendances in the 4,000s and 5,000s, are examples of teams that should indeed have been moved. The Minnesota North Stars, Winnipeg Jets, and Quebec Nordiques, with their attendances in the 15,000s, are not; so much more should have been done to keep those teams in place. Today, much as we are personally offended by the existence of the Phoenix Coyotes and Tampa Bay Lightning, the only franchise that seems ripe for a move under our criteria is the Carolina Hurricanes. They must be given a chance. But if the Hurricanes are still drawing tiny crowds and enormous apathy by 2001 or 2002, the team should be relocated somewhere where the fans are clamoring for an NHL team—or folded, thereby doing just a little to help solidify the NHL's diluted talent base.

Owners will protest that it is all well and good that the people of Winnipeg turned out in large numbers to support their team and that it was a shame the Jets had to move, but economics are economics. So they are. But with a comprehensive revenue-sharing plan in place, the so-called small-market teams would have a fighting chance to stay put, thus sparing the NHL the bad publicity that franchise moves always bring—and the alienation of Canadians, who are, after all, still the wellspring of professional hockey. When Gary Bettman became the NHL commissioner in 1993, he vowed to implement a revenue-sharing plan that would enrich all the league's teams. But after five years in office, all he was able to enact was something called the Canadian Equalization Plan, a relatively feeble, scaled-down arrangement that trickles the equivalent of pocket change (between $2 million and $6 million per team per year) to qualifying Canadian teams unable to compete with U.S. teams due to the weak Canadian dollar and the huge advantage American clubs have with their arena deals. Bettman, or somebody on the Board of Governors, must rally the votes necessary to put through a revenue-sharing plan that gives small-market teams their fair share of the wealth that they, after all, help create. Otherwise, all the statements Bettman made in 1997 and '98 to reassure a Canadian public angered by the southward exodus of its teams will ring hollow. He must back up his words with actions. To fail to do so, to allow yet another Canadian team to move to the Sun Belt, would ruin the league's already dodgy credibility and further alienate, perhaps forever, its core fans.

However, if enough votes cannot be mustered to ratify a more comprehensive revenue-sharing plan, there may be another, more coercive inducement to convince recalcitrant governors.

In the fall of 1997 a federal inquiry initiated by Dennis Mills, a Liberal MP from Toronto, brainstormed strategies for keeping NHL franchises in Calgary, Edmonton, and Ottawa healthy and in place. Canadian franchises, of course, are put at a disadvantage by U.S.-based teams, which enjoy municipal tax breaks, government-subsidized rinks, and other publicly funded goodies. The main achievement of the Mills study was in calling for hockey to be treated as a business, where it might be eligible for international trade protection from unfair competition.

In May 1998, Barry Appleton, an author and trade lawyer with practices in Toronto and New York, told Mills's group—the Heritage Canada Subcommittee on the Industry of Sports—that the United States is in violation of the North American Free Trade Agreement with respect to hockey subsidies. According to Appleton, NAFTA regulations on investment impose obligations on the federal governments of each participating country right down to the local levels. Under NAFTA, it is prohibited for a government to provide subsidies to a business in a way that gives that business an unfair advantage in international trade. Such subsidies violate the notion of "free trade" enshrined by the NAFTA agreement.

"By my understanding," Appleton told Roy MacGregor in *The Ottawa Citizen*, "hockey fits into the NAFTA definition of investment three or four different ways. But, first of all, hockey is a business, and it's a business that's worth over $1 billion a year. NAFTA specifies that you cannot give preference to a local provider of goods and services. It applies to every investment."

Appleton's advice was that the Canadian government take action on what he perceives as a clear and persistent violation of the economic accord, which would entail arranging an international panel to review the case and arbitrate any compensation. Should such a panel find against U.S.-based teams, compensation could result in a windfall of millions of dollars for Canadian teams, payable not by the NHL or the American teams or their municipalities but by the United States federal government itself—and would in all likelihood end much of the financial advantage American clubs have enjoyed.

The mobilization of NAFTA in the service of "small-market" Canadian teams may or may not be something of a long shot—but there is no question that NHL owners would not want to become embroiled in a controversy of such magnitude. Nor would the owners of U.S.-based teams want to alienate the federal, state, and local governments that subsidize their clubs through tax breaks and sweetheart arena deals. It is far likelier, under such circumstances, that big-market owners would prefer to cooperate in crafting a revenue-sharing plan to keep the small-market Canadian teams happy and healthy. Whether the impetus for adopting revenue-sharing and avoiding a NAFTA challenge comes from Bettman and progressive elements within the NHL Board of Governors, or whether it comes from outraged citizens and legislators, the goal remains the same. Small-market teams, and especially Canadian teams, must be given a much greater chance of staying put.

This brings us to the matter of teams blackmailing their cities with threats to move to greener pastures that promise grossly subsidized new buildings with luxury boxes, parking and concession revenues, and whatever else they can throw in the pot. In the NHL, a typical U.S.-team deal worked like the one in Buffalo. The Sabres made noises in the early '90s about moving out of town, and the city dutifully agreed to put up a new building to replace the municipally owned Memorial Auditorium. Although private funding paid for a far larger portion of the construction costs in Buffalo than in most cities, the new rink was nonetheless built primarily with city and state funds (which meant that hundreds of thousands of residents in New York City, who will never set foot within 300 miles of Buffalo, paid taxes to fund the arena). Upon completion, the building was turned over to the Sabres to own and operate. The City of Buffalo even had to sign an agreement stating that it would keep the fine old Aud dark, so that the new building, the Marine Midland Center, would get exclusive dibs on concerts, basketball games, and so on. Meanwhile, the Ottawa Senators had to pay out of their own pockets, as they should have, for a highway ramp leading to their new, privately funded rink on the outskirts of town.

There is no question that the Canadian way in this department is morally superior, and it is to the overwhelming credit of Canada that the public subsidization of teams—corporate welfare—is so deeply offensive north of the border. Bettman, tone deaf on this issue as he is on so many others, failed to take into account this fundamental difference between Canadian and American politics when he went to Toronto and Ottawa to lecture the public and Parliament in April 1998 on the necessity of funneling taxpayer money to Canadian teams. He got a hostile reception he could easily have avoided with a more carefully thought-out plan.

Citizens and politicians on both sides of the border should be aware that they can say no to teams when they demand more, more, more public money. Word has gotten out since the mid-'90s that despite the claims of owner-friendly politicians, who invariably say that a major league sports team adds millions upon millions of dollars to the local economy, teams in fact contribute very little if anything. "In no [U.S.] county do pro sports generate more than 0.5 percent of all jobs," according to Mark S. Rosenstraub, author of *Major League Losers: The Real Costs of Sports and Who's Paying for It*, "and the vast majority of the jobs are low-paying service sector jobs." This view is pretty much unanimous among economists and public-policy experts, and it has been widely disseminated over the past few years—so much so that voters in San Francisco, Minneapolis-St. Paul, Pittsburgh, Columbus, Houston, Seattle, and several other cities have in essence gone Canadian and voted down publicly funded stadium and arena proposals. In Wisconsin, the state legislator who cast the deciding vote in favour of building a publicly funded baseball stadium for Milwaukee was recalled by angry voters and booted out of office. Such informed skepticism on the part of American voters is encouraging, but there are still enough U.S. cities on the make—Denvers, Phoenixes, Dallases, Raleighs—willing to lure owners with huge subsidies and tax breaks.

This, once again, is where the NHL must affirm that it cares about its current fans by resisting franchise moves. Imagine how much positive attention the NHL would gather, how much good will it would generate, how much profit it could reap, simply by taking a stand against the game of franchise musical-chairs. Imagine the NHL declaring that it will stop its deadly talent-thinning expansion, that it will act to protect its small-market teams, that it will listen to its fans—and then following through on these pledges, making them league policy. The opportunity is there for the NHL, if its owners would stand up and do the right thing. The NHL—simply by saying no, we're not going to mint more useless franchises, we're *not* going to have our teams move around all the time, we're *not* going to allow the standard of play to degenerate—by being the first league to make that pledge, and then visibly working to keep it, could win back disillusioned fans, earn more new fans than it would get with a dozen more expansion teams, and gain hugely positive publicity in the United States, where now there's only negative publicity or none at all.

Whether or not the NHL manages to fix its problems with overexpansion and franchise relocation, it must still deal with a problem at least as big: what has happened to the game on the ice. The NHL must make the game on the ice fun again. *It must let hockey be hockey.* The game must be called by the rules, as it once was—tripping, holding, hooking, tackling, and every other foul must be whistled down, and it must be done consistently and constantly, no matter how much time is left in the game, who's playing, or whether it's in the early season or the Stanley Cup Final.

Even the goaltenders will tell you the NHL needs to allow its most skilful skaters to play without illegal hindrance. "You really have some great players to sell the game," said Pittsburgh's fine netminder Tom Barrasso during the '97-98 season. "We have to let the game be played for them. Until they let the great players dictate how the game is going to be played on the ice, we're going to have an inferior product. The bottom line is more attention needs to be paid to the restraining fouls. If that's done, I'm sure our game will be like it was in the early '90s— a lot of excitement and the best players really dominate."

The National Hockey League cannot afford to lose another Mario Lemieux, nor can it afford to make any other gifted skaters have to fight their way through a thorn-forest of sticks, legs, and clutching gloves before finally going down well short of the beautiful move they would otherwise have made. How many highlight-reel plays have we been deprived of over the past several years by cynical obstruction tactics, encouraged by coaches and used by checkers to hamstring talented opponents? Hockey's speed and grace and creativity are the game's greatest selling points—those qualities are what sold so many Americans on the game in the Bobby Orr era of the late '60s and the '70s, fueling the U.S. hockey boom—yet the NHL has stood by idly while those selling points have been systematically destroyed. The NHL must step up its crackdown against obstruction, not just for a month, or half a season, or for an entire season, but once and for all, no matter how many Bobby Clarkes whine about how the rules have all of a sudden been changed on him and now he has the wrong kind of team, no matter how many Don Cherrys mewl about hockey being made into a pansy sport, no matter how many retrograde coaches and commentators moan about how the parade to the penalty box is ruining the flow of the game. The game's flow is ruined already, and only the restoration of play-by-the-rules can revive it. Danny Gallivan, in a CBC Radio interview in 1989, expressed his frustration with clutch-and-grab hockey. "Call everything," he answered without hesitation when asked what needed to be done. "Call everything. The players will learn. If it takes a few weeks, or a year, or five years, they'll learn. And if takes that long, so be it. Do it anyway, and keep calling it. Because in the long run, it's what's best for hockey."

We are happy to say that in summer 1998, the NHL actually did do two things that were best for hockey. The first, of course, was an announced recommitment to the obstruction crackdown. The other was a backlash at the goaltending equipment that has enlarged exponentially since 1990. How the International Brotherhood of Goalies ever persuaded the NHL to relax the limits on the size of equipment in the first place we'll never know. Sweaters will now be of snug and practical size, no longer good for parasailing. Shoulder pads will no longer be large enough to be rented out as loft space. Gloves may now again be somewhat smaller than jai alai cestas. We're wondering why the heck they didn't pay any attention to the leg pads, the enlargement of which sparked the whole series of mutations in the first place. But we won't nitpick.

The two-referee system, although well-intentioned, doesn't seem promising. Not because the ice will be overcrowded, as some suggest, but because a consistently called game is such a rare commodity today even with only one ref. The adoption of the "Don Cherry crease"—retaining the European arc at the top of the crease, but returning to the straight sides in effect from 1951 to 1991—will have a slightly freshening effect on scoring by adding a few tap-in goals, but that will be nearly negated by increasing input from the eye in the sky. Giving the video goal judge the power to weigh in without first needing an invitation from the ref may make crease calls a bit more consistent, but it will also make them more frequent—more technology draining spontaneity from the game. Here's one case where the NHL should follow another sport's lead, and drop instant replay, as football did when the NFL acknowledged the fans' protests that the questionable gain in accuracy was more than offset by the loss in pace and excitement. Most of the other rule changes announced—tiny adjustments to the rules concerning icing, line changes, brawls, and suspensions—will have negligible effect, even the ballyhooed relocation of the goal line, from 11 to 13 feet out from the end boards.

Each small change to the rule book must be based on tradition and precedent. Profound alterations would be unthinkable in most other sports. When baseball, for instance, experienced a significant drop in batting averages in the mid-1960s, it tweaked the field of play almost imperceptibly in 1969 by lowering the height of the pitcher's mound from 15 inches to 10. It did not go insane and make baseballs the size of beachballs, change the distance between bases from 90 feet to 60, nor rule "8 strikes and yer out." There is a slippery slope out there, just a step or two beyond each ill-considered adjustment. "I'm a bit of a tradition-alist," Mark Messier said in 1997. "I think the rules of the game them-selves, the red line, the two-line pass, the offsides, things like that are something I don't think we'd ever want to take away from the game."

A word or two is in order for that vocal contingent of the hockey media that insists the solution to opening up the game lies in increas-ing the surfaces of NHL rinks to the 100-foot wide dimensions of European rinks, "because today's tremendously larger players require so much more room to operate." Trust us. You do not want to see NHL hockey on an Olympic sheet of ice. Messier speaks for most NHL stars when he says, "My experience now going over to Europe, it becomes more of a defensive game with a bigger ice surface." More defensive play is not what the NHL needs.

Fortunately, the vast international rinks are one proposed alteration to NHL play we don't have to worry much about ever seeing. Retrofitting each of 27 NHL arenas to accommodate 100-foot wide ice would entail removing six to eight 200-foot long rows of an arena's most expensive seats—about 800 of them—and the concomitant loss of that ticket revenue for every game, on top of the construction costs involved. So don't concern yourselves.

If the new set of rule changes do not succeed in restoring speed and excitement to the game, the league must go one step further. It should revert to the pre-1956-57 rule that required players to serve the full two minutes of a minor penalty, regardless of how often the team with the man advantage scored. Such a rule would make players think twice before hacking at a man or pulling him down.

Perhaps much of the aimless flailing to revise the NHL rule book is due to the unwieldy redundancy that comprises most of the rule book. Over the years, hundreds of rewordings and addenda have made the rule book a needlessly thick and confusing little volume. It's time to tidy up the NHL book. Streamline the explanations and exceptions (there's no reason on earth why "holding" and "holding the stick" should be two separate penalties with two separate rule-book entries). Then leave it alone, without additions and amendments. It has served hockey very well in pretty much its essential form since the early 1930s. Whatever's wrong with hockey now isn't because the basic rules are flawed. It's because of all the ceaseless, pointless tinkering that's done to them, and because some of the most important stuff in there is simply ignored.

Then it will only remain to give clear and unaltering instruction to NHL referees to enforce the rules the book contains. No more cracking down on one aspect of the rules while lightening up on some other section, no more focussing on this violation while forgetting about that one, only to have it all switched around next week or next year.

A game that consistently exhibits the highest levels of skill at a breakneck pace is what's best for hockey, what's best for us, the fans, and even what's best for the owners and the league. But even if the game on the ice is repaired, there's still the problem of too many games and too long a season. Even exciting, well-played hockey games become tedious if too many of them don't mean anything.

If the owners gave the shape of the season any serious thought, they'd have to realize that a shorter schedule is not only a better thing for the NHL on an aesthetic basis, it would also be better for their long-term fiscal picture. There is no question that one of the reasons for the drop in the NHL's television ratings is due to the meaninglessness of so many—almost all, really—of its regular-season games. By shortening its schedule, the NHL would add importance and drama to every one of its regular-season games. Moreover, a shorter schedule would obviate the NHL's inevitable losing battle with the NBA playoffs. Any revenue shortfall caused by fewer home games—the eternal, short-sighted rebuttal from the owners—would be more than made up for by the resulting increase in the NHL's marketability and the bigger TV contracts that would produce.

A schedule of, say, 74 games instead of the current 82 is one way to bring meaning back to the regular season. Another way is to make the regular season itself really stand for something. It should be a proud achievement for a team to finish first overall in the regular season, but these days it's dismissed as a harmful distraction from the real business at hand, winning the Stanley Cup. A lot of coaches—and, incredibly, writers and fans—think teams should not even try to win the Presidents' Trophy for best regular-season record, that they should rest key players in March and April so as to preserve their energies for the post-season.

This is a sad state of affairs, tantamount to admitting that the six months of the regular season don't count—and one the NHL can easily set right. The league ought to hype the importance of the regular season by making the Presidents' Trophy a far more celebrated achievement than it is—certainly by focusing more attention on it, and perhaps by increasing the amount of money awarded to the winning team. As in soccer around the world, where the club that finishes first over the course of a long season earns every bit as much prestige as the club that wins the cup tournament, so too should the first-place team in the NHL standings earn honour and prestige. Considering how difficult it is to maintain the highest level of play over the league's long stretch of games, there's no reason hockey's best regular-season side shouldn't command more respect for their achievement. (In fact, the league might even consider the money-spinning possibilities of holding a one-game, winner-take-all Presidents' Trophy game at the end of the regular season between the Eastern Conference champion and Western Conference champion, to be held in the building of the team with the better record. A one-game final in front of a packed house and a national TV audience, with glory and maybe $500,000 on the line—now *that* would be fun to watch.)

Another obvious way to enhance the importance of the regular season is by adjusting the home-ice advantage for playoff teams according to the teams' regular-season records. Why should a team that finishes 30 or 40 points ahead of its playoff opponent earn only the meagre advantage of a single home game? Give the team that finishes a mile ahead of its playoff adversary all seven games at home, or at least six out of seven. Scale it down to five and two for a more moderate advantage in the standings, and leave four and three for the closest races. Now you've got regular-season games being contested not just to make the playoff cut, but to earn a tangible bonus for playing consistent top-flight hockey all season long. And with a revenue-sharing plan in place, the team with just one or two home playoff games would still get a fair piece of the profits.

These solutions do not address the Gordian knot formed by 27 (soon 30) NHL teams—an apt metaphor, because the only workable solutions involve just that, cutting the league in two. There are too many teams and too many players to keep track of anymore, even for avid fans. And the bloated number of teams means most clubs won't play other clubs more than once or twice a year. Traditional rivalries have died out—we now live in a world where the Toronto Maple Leafs play the Detroit Red Wings exactly once a year—and if four divisions were too many for a fan to keep straight, what does that say about six divisions?

The answer to this mess is to divide the NHL into two entirely separate entities—into, for all practical purposes, two distinct and manageable leagues of 15 teams each. Two leagues of that size, still fully under the control of and operated by the National Hockey League, would eliminate much of the anonymity that plagues hockey today and return a sense of familiarity—and intensity—for fans and players.

But which teams to divide into which leagues? That's easy. Fans in Montreal and Toronto have no interest in watching the Nashville Predators and the Carolina Hurricanes; they want to see the Red Wings and the Blackhawks. And fans in Nashville and Carolina don't know about or care about the traditions that the Canadiens and Maple Leafs represent; they're just as happy to watch the Lightning and the Sharks. So, divide the NHL accordingly, by the date of a city's entry. One league, call it the Prince of Wales League, would be composed of the traditional Old Guard clubs, the pre-1975 teams, and one of the more recent, post-'75, expansion franchises. The other league, call it the Campbell League, would be made up of new clubs.

Basically the two leagues might shake out along these lines:

Prince of Wales League	Campbell League
Montreal ('17)	Edmonton ('79)
Toronto ('17)	Calgary ('80)
Boston ('24)	New Jersey ('82)
Detroit ('26)	San Jose ('91)
Chicago ('26)	Tampa Bay ('92)
N.Y. Rangers ('26)	Dallas ('93)
Pittsburgh ('67)	Anaheim ('93)
St. Louis ('67)	Florida ('93)
Philadelphia ('67)	Colorado ('95)
Los Angeles ('67)	Phoenix ('96)
Buffalo ('70)	Carolina ('97)
Vancouver ('70)	Nashville ('98)
N.Y. Islanders ('72)	Atlanta ('99)
Washington ('74)	Columbus ('00)
Ottawa ('17/'92)	Minnesota ('00)

There's room for compromise and special considerations, based on rivalry or geography, but we're sure you see the advantages. Two 15-team leagues mean fans and players will know all about all the other teams in the league, and that rivalries will grow and grow fierce. Best of all, you'd see the teams you care about most—or hate most, actually—far more often. Each league could be divided into two or three divisions and have its own playoffs. Then the two league playoff champions could meet in the Stanley Cup Final, carrying not just the banner of their city but of the league they represent as well.

We kind of doubt whether the NHL is willing to undertake a makeover this radical, but the point remains: the league must shorten regular-season and playoff schedules, and it must do something to restore rivalries and end the anonymity caused by too many teams and too many players spread out over too many places.

Regardless of how many teams play how many games, the experience of *attending* games has to be improved. The NHL currently permits teams to blast bone-jarring canned rock at us during stoppages in play. This practice should be ended immediately, or at the very least, strict limits should be applied to volume levels in every arena. It's painful, destroys any chance for fans to cheer, boo, or converse, and ruins the atmosphere in general. (Stop them before they go the way of Pro Beach Hockey and start cranking "We Will We Will Rock You" *while play is in progress!*). It's we, the fans, who should be responsible for any deafening dins being raised at the hockey game, not some psychopathic arena minion with a soundboard and a pile of audiotapes.

The league should also override the petty, fragile egos of individual club brass and reinstate the fans' right to hang any damn sign or banner they want, a practice that for years now has been banned at many NHL rinks. Didn't know that? You say you still see hand-painted banners hanging at lots of rinks when you watch on TV? Yeah, that fooled us too for a while. Then it occurred to us they were all the same size, all painted in the same style, and that none of them were ever remotely

clever or had a single critical thing to say about the team or its management. Try hanging a sign suggesting that one of your last-place
team's go-through-the-motions players be traded, or that the owner or
the GM is a nitwit. Security people will soon arrive to take it away,
telling you it's obstructing someone's view. Just one more brick in the
wall being built to separate the fans from the game.

The fans' passion for the game, for their team, is to be embraced, not
feared and muzzled. Has any recent confrontation between fans and
management better illustrated the NHL's attitude toward its customers
than the lawsuit Bill Wirtz and the Blackhawks brought to shut down
the brilliant, carping Chicago fanzine, *The Blue Line*? As we write this,
Blue Line continues to fight the good fight in court against the
Blackhawks' greedy, thin-skinned ownership.

What about the rinks themselves? As long as new arenas are popping
up like mushrooms, how about actually making them fan-friendly,
instead of just proclaiming them fan-friendly and hoping fans are hyp-
notized into believing it? Because of modern building codes, there's only
so much you can do to give them the look and feel and character of
hockey's old cathedrals. But wouldn't an effort toward that end be great?
The owners might take notice of how profitable this very idea has
proven in baseball. In the 1960s and '70s, the diamond game, like
hockey in the '80s and '90s, abandoned and destroyed the charming,
idiosyncratic old ballparks teams had played in for decades, and con-
structed enormous, antiseptic, virtually identical stadiums throughout
the major leagues. Fans hated them, and pined for Ebbets Field, Forbes
Field, and dozens of other classic ballparks. But the Baltimore Orioles

went the opposite way when they replaced their stadium in the late '80s; bucking the trend of huge, faceless, "state-of-the-art" stadia, they built Camden Yards, a quirky, beautiful, intimate ballpark that was an architectural paean to the fields of yesteryear. The place won every laurel and measure of esteem it's possible for a stadium to receive, from architects and critics to the fans themselves. It still draws fans by the thousands from out of town to experience the intimacy of baseball in an old-fashioned park. Cleveland and the Dallas area followed Baltimore's lead, and both are reaping many of the same benefits as Baltimore, including a steady supply of sellout crowds.

Would it be such a leap of imagination to consider making the next hockey arena to be built an *hommage* to the great buildings of the past? Put a little effort into the facade to distinguish it from a suburban industrial park. Beef up the interior structure, tighten the space and darken the colours, to distinguish it from any airy, pastel shopping mall. Make the seating as tight and steep as the law will allow to pack in crowds and afford them decent sight lines. Limit the seating to an intimate 16,000 or 17,000 instead of a 25,000-seat megabuilding filled with banks of empty seats. Make sure the inevitable luxury suites are as outwardly unobtrusive as possible. Every effort must be made to construct them in a way that does no violence to the seating and sight lines of everyone else in the building. Only then can the passionate atmosphere of a hockey game be restored.

The importance of atmosphere at a game cannot be overestimated. The electricity generated by knowledgable, fervent fans packed chock-a-block into marvellous historic arenas was a wondrous thing to experience—and it was one more thing that sold hockey to Americans in the late '60s and early '70s. Americans unfamiliar with hockey saw how much more involved and passionate hockey fans were than baseball, football, or basketball fans. That electric thrill of attending a raucous, emotionally consuming hockey game—an atmosphere made possible not by electronic scoreboards and canned music, but by chanting, singing fans, multitudes of homemade banners, and peals of cheers, boos, ooohs and aahhhs—helped create the U.S. hockey boom.

If the atmosphere at NHL games can be restored to what it was—a fan-generated, passionate, heartfelt thing—it, too, would serve to increase hockey's appeal. Hey owners! Atmosphere is yet another selling point that works. Give the arena experience back to the fans. Everyone will be the richer for it.

Everywhere in the game, artistic sense seems as lacking as hockey sense or business sense. The NHL is desperately in need of stronger quality-control standards to guide the way teams look. What teams wear—and even worse, what some of them call themselves—is an embarrassment to the game.

When a franchise pays its expansion fee, it hasn't purchased the right to help make hockey a bush-league laughingstock. When some new team decides its nickname is going to be *The Wild* or *The Frenzy*, the NHL, instead of approving it, has to stand up and say *no—try again*. When a team decides its crest is going to feature yet another generic carnivore with a rabid snarl or a cuddly cartoon animal cradling a hockey stick or an abstract Rorschach test of swirling colour, or anything at all downloaded off a computer clip-art file, the NHL has to say *no—try again*. When any team decides its seventh new sweater design in three years will have a colour scheme featuring teal and turquoise zigzags and puce and fuschia polka dots on base black, the NHL has to say *no—try again*. New names, sweaters, and crests should be made subject to league approval by a panel of artists and designers whose most important credentials are that they're life-long hockey fans. That way, any changes that are made will remain within the context of the game's traditions (bravo to the Islanders for dumping their seasick fisherman and returning to the uniforms of their glory years). And like coins and currency, limits should be placed on how often designs can be changed. The constant parade of new togs is a major contributor to the impression of chaos and instability that plagues the NHL.

The league and its component clubs should also take a stronger hand in ensuring that the language of the game is not irretrievably corrupted. The NHL should hasten to restore the conference and division names that attested to the game's history, for a start. How does the league talk about itself and (when it talks about it at all) about its past? Press releases should adhere to a simple league-issued style book that would forbid obnoxious imports from other sports and stress the use of proper hockey language. No more quarterbacking the power play, drafting of power forwards, or knuckleballing wrist shots. Hockey is hockey, not football, basketball, or baseball.

NHL owners have never understood that it's the romance of the game—the traditions, the legacy, the character, the emotion—that builds fan loyalty. That's nothing to sneeze or snicker at. It's often what draws fans to a sport and more important, it's always what involves them and keeps them coming back. It's what elevates a major sport above a designer sport. For baseball fans, it's not just a bunch of guys standing around on a big field, without context or associations; it's a timeless moment filled with everything baseball's ever been—Babe Ruth, Mickey Mantle, the smell of linseed oil on a glove, the Black Sox, the colour line, Gehrig's farewell speech, the '62 Mets, Roberto Clemente, having a catch with Dad and Gramps, 61, .401, 714. For football fans, it's Joe Montana, the Refrigerator, Ron Lancaster and Sam "the Rifle" Etcheverry, high school marching bands and majorettes, Ray Nitschke, Darryl Stingley, the Immaculate Reception, the Grey Cup parade, 2003, 73-0, 17-and-0. Even most basketball fans know something about Cousy and Havlicek, Chamberlain and Russell, Earl the Pearl, Earl the Goat, Showtime, and the Fab Five. The point is that in every other major sport, all of that's there, every game, on the field, at the stadium, on every broadcast on TV and radio, all the time, with the insistence of the league itself; every fan is brought not just into the game at hand, but into the continuum of the sport. A game doesn't stand as an isolated event, it's made part of an immense chain of events, the newest chapter in a living history, the culmination of everything that's gone before.

Where does that exist in hockey? Canadians and veteran fans in the northern United States play and watch and listen to the game with the Rocket, the China Wall, Foster Hewitt, Roger Doucet, the Renfrew Creamery Kings, the Trail Smoke Eaters, Ted Green, Tiger Williams, Bill Masterton, 50 in 50, right there with them. But in the rest of

America, where a loyal fan base is crucial to the NHL's success but where hockey has all the resonance of any fly-by-night designer sport, none of those things have any meaning, none of them even exist, not on a broadcast, not at the arena, not in the culture. Ask a new hockey fan who Ted Lindsay or Ted Kennedy or Jean Beliveau were, let alone King Clancy or Newsy Lalonde, and they'll look at you as if you'd just asked them to name all the Dalai Lamas since 1650.

The NHL must turn from deliberately ignoring its history to aggressively promoting and celebrating that history. The creation of a department modeled on NFL Films, a stronger partnership with the Hockey Hall of Fame, insisting that both network and local broadcasts get this material in front of American fans, installing display space in the concourses of new arenas to mount eye-catching exhibits on the history of the game—these are just a few obvious first steps the NHL should waste no time in taking. By celebrating its legends, lore, and tradition, by stressing the sense of being part of a continuum of adventure and excellence—the NHL can draw people not just to the game but *into* the game, so that they stay, so that they become fans and remain fans.

However much Canadians might be saddened by the loss of their status as the outright, absolute No. 1 nation in the world of hockey, there is no question that the spread of excellent hockey throughout the world is a good thing. International competition brings a whole new level of passion, excitement, and attention to the game, and the NHL should recognize the benefits it reaps from that heightened interest. Some naysayers will always protest that an international tournament not won by Canada or the United States is a failure, but they are wrong and must be ignored. Everyone benefits from a top-level world tournament.

The NHL, therefore, must reaffirm its commitment to full participation in the Olympics. It must continue to make room in its schedule (which is too long anyway) for an Olympic break, and it must insist that its member clubs release all players involved for all Olympic qualifying and final-round games. Furthermore, the league must improve on its World Cup tournament. It must make it a wintertime event instead of a summertime event, so that it can capture the attention of the media. And, rather than holding the tournament in North America each time, every other World Cup should be held in Europe, not just to make it a fair test of each nation's skill, but to grow the game on that continent as well.

As a billion-dollar industry, as the prime force in all of hockey, the NHL has the power to set trends and policy, and the responsibility to use that power to positively influence all the hockey around it and below it. When the game was disgraced by the sex abuse scandals at Maple Leaf Gardens and in Swift Current, was there any official response beyond a few embarrassed mutterings to the effect of *gee, that's pretty awful?* and a small contribution to Sheldon Kennedy's charity rollerblade trek across Canada? Just as when the prevalence of alcoholism among players started taking up more inches in the sports pages, the NHL looked off into space and remained quiet. And now again, with grim reports of sexual predators victimizing youth players and young fans, another opportunity is being wasted—not just to enhance the NHL's image with a decisive, positive response, but much more important, to make an actual contribution to the welfare of hockey and the kids who play it by proposing sensible new guidelines for youth hockey to adopt.

Trumpeting a position paper that emphasizes a renewed focus on parental responsibility, coaching qualifications, and background checks on anyone associated with youth hockey programs is the obvious place for the NHL to start. And the league could do so much more: recommend that all youth players right up through juniors play only for a team within, say, 100 miles of their home town, or recommend an end to the trading of players. Or, on a more immediate basis, the NHL could take the lead in developing counselling services for the kids, using a small portion of the profits made in junior and pro hockey. Such a plan—a sort of employee assistance program for adolescent players—would help monitor all youth leagues, discourage predators, dispense information, report violations, and advise the kids. The NHL would do well by doing good. The benefits to the league's image would be great. The benefits to hockey and the kids who play it would be even greater.

There is another area in which the NHL would benefit from taking a brave, principled stance: fighting. The game's image in the United States is unnecessarily tarnished because it continues to allow fighting—it may be the No. 1 reason why the NHL's efforts to grow the game in the States have faltered. How many millions of dollars in American TV money, merchandising, and franchise fees have NHL owners thrown away by their insistence on propping up fighting? But more important, how many fine youth players on both sides of the border have hung up their skates because of all the mindless violence in the junior leagues? How many parents have steered their children away from a career in hockey because they don't want to see their son's face punched in, or their son punching someone else's face in? Hockey is unique and wonderful and rugged enough without needing goonery and fisticuffs to differentiate itself from the rest of the pack. The NHL should fall in line with every other sport in the world and eject players who fight. When a fight breaks out, the linesmen must step in at the first opportunity and break it up, and the referee must send the players off for the rest of the game—and the next game as well. A particularly egregious fight or instigation of a fight must result in an even longer suspension. We know, we know—as we said earlier, we like a good mix-up, particularly that rarest kind of fight: an honest scrap born of real anger. But if that must be sacrificed in order to stamp out the embarrassing freak show of premeditated goonery, so be it.

Not just goonery, but stick-swinging violence and the deliberate intent to injure must be wiped out as well. Some of that would be accomplished by the kind of close refereeing and recommitment to the rule book we have been promised. But the National Hockey League Players Association must also step up for the good of the game and for its own self-interest. The NHLPA has been silent about violence issues far too long, allowing the careers of too many of its members to be harmed or curtailed by the reckless actions of their union brothers. When one NHLPA member deliberately or recklessly injures another, the union must speak out to censure the act and the member who perpetrated it. The players must learn that union brothers ought to treat each other with respect—or, at the very least, do nothing that might shorten the career of a fellow union member.

Finally, there is something all of us, as fans, must do. For years faceless men in corporate suites have moved our teams away from our cities, torn down our favourite rinks, jacked up ticket prices, charged usurious fees for "extras" like parking and eating undercooked hot dogs, changed team colours and crests that we loved for generations, drowned us out and stupefied us with constant high-decibel assaults through PA systems and giant scoreboards, muzzled us by banning homemade signs, drained the drama from our favourite sport with overlong regular-season and playoff schedules and too many damn teams. In short, we have been treated like dirt. But we have not done much about it beyond muttering and griping.

We fans must learn to protest in a more organized fashion whenever something bad is done to us. It is a long-standing tradition overseas, especially in soccer, where fans organize protests (nonviolent ones, believe it or not) outside the offices of team directors or in the stadium itself. The fans come together to show their club that, no, they do *not* approve of their top player being sold to another club; no, they do *not* want their beloved stadium demolished in favour of a cookie-cutter replacement; no, they do *not* want the men who run their club incompetently to continue serving on the board. And these protests do indeed work sometimes, usually by exposing the greed of the men in charge and embarrassing them into acting like good citizens. Hockey fans can and must organize and protest in this way too. The next time your team makes noises about raising prices yet again, or changing your team's crest into some mauve-and-eggplant-shaded flesh-render, or confiscates your sign that says your coach must go—organize! Get your friends and neighbours in your section to *all* bring signs to the next game. Start a chant, and if the p.a. drowns it out, chant while play is in progress. Get a little picket line going for an hour or two in front of the building. Start a zine or an Internet message board and take the piss out of the suits who fleece you just because you love hockey and your hometown team.

This may sound impossibly idealistic, but in fact it has already happened in the NHL. The incredible protest movement begun and sustained by Winnipeg Jets fans in the mid-'90s was one of the most inspiring episodes in the history of North America fandom. Ultimately it did not work, and the Jets wound up departing their weeping fans in an unforgettably poignant final farewell. But the positive results of the Jets fans' uprising were many: it kept the team in Winnipeg an extra year; it involved all of Canada in a dramatic outpouring of sympathy and support, as even children in far-off provinces donated lunch money and allowances to the Jets' cause; and it finally threw into sharp relief just how ruinous the policies of the NHL really are. Perhaps most important, it let owners know that they could no longer count on yanking teams around the map without a peep from hockey fans. Oilers fans may owe the continuing existence of their team in Edmonton to the awareness created by the protests of Winnipeg fans. Those fans made quite a commotion, and the positive effects of that commotion are still being heard today. The Winnipeg Jets did not die in vain.

But we fans must remain on guard, so that the stirring example of

Winnipeg fans is not forgotten. When something is done to hurt hockey, we must do more than grumble and whinge amongst ourselves. We must learn to say *no*—loudly, clearly, unmistakably. The legacy forged by men like Cyclone Taylor, King Clancy, Howe and Richard, Orr and Gretzky, must not be squandered. Our game must not be allowed to dwindle away to a quaint lost folk-art understood and remembered only by a handful of eccentric admirers. We must not allow our teams and their history to be taken away from us by corporate suits who don't give a damn and who treat the game and its fans like a money machine. We must not allow our game to be undermined, cheapened, distorted, or humiliated. We must not allow hockey to die.

The game *can* be saved. It *can* be made better than it is now. It can again be made as great as it once was. All that's required are the same things that have always won in hockey—swift action, anticipation, self-lessness, cooperation, communication, the ability to take a hit, good sense, smart moves, and a strong will. If the men who control hockey can dig deep and find those abilities in themselves, in the end, they, the fans, and the game itself all win.

the hockey fan's manifesto, 1998-99

WE, THE LOYAL AND PASSIONATE HOCKEY FANS OF CANADA AND THE UNITED STATES, are deeply disturbed by the state our beloved sport finds itself in today. National Hockey League games, once filled with excitement, drama, and fun, have been robbed of those qualities by:

- rampant overexpansion;
- the removal of teams from traditional centres;
- turgid play on the ice;
- the abandonment of classic, tradition-rich rinks;
- management policies that foul the experience of attending games and silence fans;
- a general contempt for hockey tradition;
- the continued refusal to control violent play; and
- the inescapable impression that the NHL cares nothing for long-time fans, and that potential new fans in regions with no hockey tradition are to be wooed at all costs.

IVEN THESE URGENT PROBLEMS which threaten the economic well-being of teams, the aesthetics of the game and hockey itself, we urge the National Hockey League to join with the NHL Players Association and make hockey whole and healthy again by taking the following steps:

1. Enact an immediate moratorium on further expansion.
2. Stop the southward exodus of teams.
3. Install a meaningful revenue-sharing plan.
4. Fix the game on the ice by calling it by the rule book.
5. Control excessive violence and abolish fighting.
6. Reject all suggestion for absurd rule changes.
7. Abolish video reviews.
8. Shorten the schedule.
9. Increase the reward for regular-season excellence.
10. Restore team rivalries.
11. Restore the arena experience and revive the ambiance of the classic rinks.
12. Respect and celebrate hockey's traditions.
13. Reaffirm the commitment to international hockey.
14. Become a force for moral good at all levels of the game.
15. Listen to and accept the criticism of the fans.

And finally we fans must speak out and organize and protest whenever the NHL or club owners act in a way contrary to our best interests or that of the game itself. Say it loud—they're our teams. It's our game.